THE INTENTIONAL PARENTING PLAN

TIPP

VEDA PENDLETON MCCLAIN, PH.D.

authorHOUSE®

AuthorHouse™
1663 Liberty Drive
Bloomington, IN 47403
www.authorhouse.com
Phone: 1-800-839-8640

First published by AuthorHouse 9/15/2009

ISBN: 978-1-4389-9741-4 (e)
ISBN: 978-1-4389-9740-7 (sc)

Printed in the United States of America
Bloomington, Indiana

This book is printed on acid-free paper.

DEDICATION

● ● ● ● ● ● ● ● ● ● ● ● ● ● ● ● ●

To my mother, Jimmie Lee Pendleton (1926-2008), who was truly my transformer before the notion of transforming ever occurred to me. She also worked to transform the lives of strangers who became her friends.

Acknowledgements

. . . .

"Teach the older women to be reverent in the way they live, not to be slanderers or addicted to much wine, but to teach what is good. Then they can train the younger women to love their husbands and children, to be self-controlled and pure, to be busy at home, to be kind, and to be subject to their husbands, so that no one can malign the word of God." Titus 2:3-5

God given and God driven is the best descriptor for this work. Although I have parented for over 30 years, the idea for this work came to me about two years ago near the birth of my oldest daughter's first son. At that time, I asked her if she had a plan for his life. She asked me what I meant and I told her that she needed a written plan for his life. I, then, began to sketch on an envelope what I thought such a plan would look like. It was not until 18 months later that God impressed upon me the need to get more on paper. So, this is a God project.

I thank God for giving me this idea that has the potential to help parents in rearing their children. Throughout my parenting years, God has blessed me with the knowledge, skills, and disposition to rear my children in a Christian loving environment, one that I and other members of my immediate family and friends helped to create for them. I do not claim to have had all of the answers. I did, however, have the support and benefit of the collective wisdom of the mothers, grandmothers, aunts, and other mothers who surrounded us and supported us. As a younger woman, I was trained by the older women how to love, train, and care for my children. To them, I am eternally grateful.

Thank you to those who read drafts of TIPP and provided valuable feedback, including Nicole Allen, Gail Hollamon, Dr. Bonnie Marshall and Nyoka Woods. Your insight and words of wisdom helped me complete the process.

I also thank my children (Marian, Lauren, David, Jennifer, and Micah) who gave me the experiences about which I now write. They have challenged me to grow and develop in ways that I had not planned. They also made me think about the many gifts and talents each person brings to our world and how those gifts and talents are special and designed for a specific purpose in meeting a need in the kingdom of God.

Finally, to my friends who have cheered me on to develop and write this plan. Thanks for your encouragement and love.

TABLE OF CONTENTS

● ●

PREFACE

● ● ● ● ● ● ● ● ● ● ● ● ● ● ● ● ● ● ● ●

The first intentional parenting plan was written for Jesus by God through the prophets who foretold His coming. God did not send Jesus to earth without a written plan for His life from conception to birth, and from birth to death and His subsequent reign on high. The scriptures foretold the coming of Christ for centuries before He was born. In foretelling the coming of Christ, the prophets wrote about Him and gave us specific details as to the plan God had for the life of Jesus, the Christ. God did not leave Christ's birth, death, and resurrection up to hope and chance. God had a plan, and in His infinite wisdom, He chose to have prophets write the vision for the life of Christ. Their writings prepared the way for His arrival, established His purpose for coming, and published His character. In clearly written language, God gave us the plan for the life of Christ and His purpose (Jeremiah 23:5-6).

The prophet Isaiah told us of His heritage (Isaiah 11:1-2) and Matthew confirmed it (Matthew1) by giving the lineage of Christ that led to His birth. We were also told where He would be born (Micah 5:2-4) and that His mother would be a virgin (Isaiah 7:14, Luke 1:26-37). God even told us what His name would be and what He would be called (Matthew 1:21-23; Luke 1:31-33; Philippians 2:9-11). The roles He would play on earth were given (Isaiah 9:6-7) and they matched the subsequent actions that He would take. His character was described (Isaiah 11: 3-5) long before He came to be.

Further plans for His life were given about what He would do (Isaiah 49:1-7; Daniel 7:14; Luke 1:32-33), how He would live (Isaiah 42:1-4), and how He would change the world (Psalm 72:8-9, 11-17). Finally, even Christ's death was part of the written plan for His coming to earth. Isaiah (25:8) foretells His suffering and death (Isaiah 53:1-12) and even His resurrection (Isaiah 25:8).

God knew that there needed to be a plan for the Christ child. It needed to be a thorough written plan that told the world what God the Father envisioned for the life of Christ. He was deliberate in planning Jesus Christ's life and specific in what He wanted Christ to do on earth. He planned the life of Jesus Christ long before Jesus Christ arrived on the scene. God articulated His vision for Jesus in a way that gave meaning and purpose to the life of Jesus. Through that purpose, Jesus was able to know and understand just why He came to earth, and why it was necessary for Him to live, suffer and die as He did. His sense of purpose drew Him to the things of

God with love and understanding and helped Him in His daily walk. Because Jesus knew what His purpose was, He was able to fulfill it. He came to fulfill the law about which the prophets had written.

And so it should be when we plan the lives of our children. We should write a plan that shows our understanding of the child's purpose. We should be deliberate and specific, and we should plan as much in advance as we can. We should spend time praying, thinking, and reflecting on the life that we want each child to live, and how that child's life can and will impact the world. As parents, we should further be able to understand our roles in the parenting process and how our actions can and will shape the life of the child. Finally, as we parent, we should continually seek God's wisdom about how we should parent, and ask Him to help us be the kind of parent He would have us to be for each child.

*"Therefore everyone who hears these words of mine and puts them into practice is like a wise man who built his house on the rock. The rain came down, the streams rose, and the winds blew and beat against that house; yet it did not fall, because it had its foundation on the rock. But everyone who hears these words of mine and does not put them into practice is like a foolish man who built his house on sand. The rain came down, the streams rose, and the winds blew and beat against that house, and it fell with a great crash." **Matthew 7:24-27***

BEGINNING TO THINK AND PLAN

• •

"Whatever is true, whatever is noble, whatever is right, whatever is pure, whatever is lovely, whatever is admirable, if anything is excellent or praiseworthy, think about such things." Philippians 4:8

"Therefore everyone who hears these words of mine and puts them into practice is like a wise man who built his house on the rock. The rain came down, the streams rose, and the winds blew and beat against that house; yet it did not fall, because it had its foundation on the rock. But everyone who hears these words of mine and does not put them into practice is like a foolish man who built his house on sand. The rain came down, the streams rose, and the winds blew and beat against that house, and it fell with a great crash." Matthew 7:24-27

"I will show you what he is like who comes to me and hears my words and put them into practice. He is like a man building a house, who dug down deep and laid the foundation on rock. When a flood came, the torrent struck that house but could not shake it, because it was well built. But the one who hears my words and does not put them into practice is like a man who built a house on the ground without a foundation. The moment the torrent struck that house, it collapsed and its destruction was complete." Luke 6:47-49

No one begins building a house without giving serious consideration to the plans for building it. The plans serve as directions for how the house will be built, where each room will be located, how big the rooms will be, and what materials will be used in constructing the house. Within the plans are additional plans for the foundation, electrical wiring, plumbing, flooring, wall materials, lighting, roofing, etc. that make it clear to the builders just how the contractor or the owner wants the finished product to look. Those plans call for careful thought about how and where each feature of the house will be and how it will look as well as an estimated budget for building the house. Even with those clearly and carefully designed plans, there are flaws in materials and sometimes even in workmanship due to human error and frailty. Nothing that is manmade is perfect, and it can never be perfect.

The same is true of designing and building cars, computers, telephones, furniture, bridges, televisions, and any other manmade creation. Wherever there is a creation, a plan was first created and developed with careful consideration of the proposed product or outcome and its potential usage. In each case, the designer had or has a plan.

In business, there are organizational charts, vision and mission statements, along with strategic plans that chart the course for the company. These plans have specific goals, a timeline, and actions outlined so that members of the organization can know, understand, and follow the company's plans. These plans exist for purpose and clarity of mission so that the desired outcome is reached. Although such plans are common and expected in manmade creations and organizations, most of us rarely if ever think of having such a plan for child rearing, and therefore, do not plan as intensely or intentionally for the lives of our children.

Creating and Rearing Children

Creating and rearing children should involve intense and intentional planning before, during, and after the birth of the child. This planning should begin with an idea of the purpose for the family and for the child. From that sense of purpose should emerge a plan for the growth and development of the child as a contributing member of the family.

Creating and rearing children is not always planned, and even when parents prepare for the birth of a child, rarely do they take the time and actually plan and write down their plans for rearing the child. Many parents have indicated that they do not have a written plan, a plan that someone else could pick up and implement in the event of a catastrophic illness, prolonged absence, or even death. Most parents have ideas about how they would want their child to be reared, but no one to date has acknowledged having a thoughtfully written plan for their child. Just like in building a house, there are plans, parents need specific plans for what they would ideally like to see happen in the lives of their children that will help them grow and develop into successful adults.

The Intentional Parenting Plan

The Intentional Parenting Plan (TIPP) is the beginning of such a plan for parents as they work to rear their children. I truly believe that each parent does the best that he/she knows to do with their child. They do the best with the knowledge, understanding, and faith that they have. When more knowledge is gained in a particular area, parents begin to make the necessary changes that are in the best interests of their child. Many times because of a lack of understanding, parents, like other humans, sometimes make choices and decisions that are not in the best interests of their child. These decisions sometimes send the family spiraling out of control or at least in an undesirable direction, and it takes months and sometimes years for the family situation to be remedied and reconciled in meaningful ways that turn around a poor decision.

TIPP is an attempt to help parents think, reflect, and make thoughtful decisions through planning ahead for what they want to see happen in the life of each child; that is, before a decision is made about the rearing of the child. This is not an easy task, nor is it one that should be taken lightly or done in haste. Thoughtful planning and decision-making requires a combination of close self-examination, prayer, knowledge, and insight into human nature. These are all aspects of life that affect who we become as we interact with others in the world. In other words, there are no easy answers and there is no single answer that will work for every child or family. Even children within the same household will have differing emotional, spiritual, educational, physical, and disciplinary needs that parents will need to consider as they develop and write their child-rearing plans. As you think and plan for rearing your child, explore whatever is Godly. The Apostle Paul encourages us to think on ideas that are "noble, true, right, pure, lovely, admirable, excellent, or praiseworthy" as we live our lives. And so it is ideas that can be described as such that we should use as we develop our plans. These are the essentials that are needed in order to rear godly children.

TIPP is only the beginning, and it will change as the needs of your family grow and change. Like other parents, I did not have a written plan as my older children were growing up, but with time and experiences, I began to make plans on paper, sometimes on napkins or envelopes that guided my thinking and actions in child-rearing. That lack prompted this plan.

My Plan

Early when my oldest child was still a toddler, I began to realize that I was going to have to plan her life. It meant that any plans that I made for my life had to include thoughts and ideas about how my plans would affect her life. The plans became a plan, a plan for me and my family.

It would be many years before I would ever write down any plans, but I always kept a mental image of what I wanted an adult child of mine to look like. I knew that success in school was important. I knew that I wanted each child to have a relationship with Jesus. I knew that I wanted each child to value relationships and people over material possessions. I also knew that there were core values that I wanted each child to have that could and would transcend time and place. These were core values that I had been taught as a child and they were the ones that have served as my guide and propellers in life.

And so, in every situation as I studied each child, I began to make mental plans for their lives and what I hoped they would look like as adults. I studied the situation and each child and what I needed to do as the parent in order to shape the child's behavior and response in the situation. In observing the child, I was challenged to think about the child's natural inclination and what would be needed to properly shape the will and actions of the child. I also thought about how I would want the child to behave in my absence should a similar situation occur again. I decided I wanted the child to be prepared to respond and to act appropriately to any situation by thinking first and learning to keep their heads in all situations.

My plans consisted of prioritizing people and then other activities and possessions. Church and family were first. School and getting an education were second. Extra-curricular activities and friends were third, and television and video games were last. Time was allotted for each area of the plan depending on the priority placement on the list, with church, family, and school taking up the bulk of the time.

This worked for my family. There is no silver bullet or wisdom in a bottle that guarantees anything about a human being. There are way too many variables, distractions, and frailties in humanity to guarantee success. There are, however, some basics that could form a firm foundation for positive human growth and development. These basics are the rock, the firm foundation that serves to keep us focused and well through any situation. That foundation must be rooted and grounded in someone who is greater than we are. That someone is Jesus Christ. These basics are the source of the development of this plan. By thinking through the answers to questions about issues parents face daily, parents can begin for formulate a plan for child rearing. This plan can and will provide parents with answers before a situation arises.

Matthew and Luke tell us the importance of building our houses on the rock, the firm foundation of a life in Christ. And so it is in child rearing that we should plan and build the lives of our children on the teachings that we get from the word of God. It is only through God's word that we are able to get clear directions for our lives and for those of our children.

"Commit to the Lord whatever you do, and your plans will succeed." **Proverbs 16:3**

Your Plans

Even with the best planned life, there are bumps in the road. Most of us would like to think of our lives as orderly and well planned. The reality is that many times we do not take the time to plan and to think through what we really want to see happen in our lives or in the lives of our children. We say that we are taking life as "one day at a time" and so we lock ourselves into thinking that we are supposed to live our lives in such a manner without written plans for daily living. We are not supposed to fret or worry about our lives in ways that show a lack of faith in God's ability to provide for us, but we are supposed to have an idea of how we want to live our lives and to make plans that show that we have vision and purpose for our existence.

Parenting is the most difficult job because it requires that you use your heart and head in making decisions about your own flesh that resides in a different body that is equipped with its own personality, talents, strengths, weaknesses, and free will. As parents, we do have an endless source that we can access in the parenting process, and that source is the Word of God.

Using scriptures, this is a compilation of the mantras, thoughts, and ideas I have chosen to implement in my child-rearing. Unfortunately, I did not have a pre-prepared written guide to which I could refer as I made daily decisions. I now wonder what would have happened to my children had I passed away before they reached adulthood. Who would have known what my wishes were in rearing them or what I hoped to see them become? I also did not have the biblical insight that God has given me over the years with regard to parenting and living. Here is an opportunity for you to develop a written plan for your child.

This planning document is by no means the final authority on child-rearing. It is, however, a beginning to think about, explore, and start to implement that which you think will help your child become the human being you want to see. Beginning with the adult child in mind, this plan will help you carefully articulate the steps that you want to take and make in growing and developing your child. And so it has been through faith that I have put these words on paper to share in the child-rearing process with parents and guardians who have not yet begun to put their ideas about their child on paper.

Purpose of TIPP

Most parents spend more time planning a child's first birthday party than they do in planning for any area of the child's life, including spiritual training and education. Many of us take for granted that there will always be enough time and enough information available to us in order for us to make sound on-the-spot decisions. Many vital decisions in child-rearing are left open to chance; a chance that we will make the right decision; a chance that our child will grow up and become the person we desire that they become; a chance that others will interact in positive and meaningful ways with our child; and a chance that our child will learn to plan her/his own life.

We take these chances, not because we do not care enough to plan our child-rearing practices, but because no one has ever really challenged us to pause long enough to think about and to think through what it means to parent intentionally with a specific purpose in mind. Nor do we fully understand how to channel all of our talents, skills, abilities, dispositions, and energies in one direction for the general well-being and growth and development of our child. We want the best for each child, but rarely do we know how to plan for that best and then how to take the appropriate steps to implement those plans. We are rarely sure about what needs to come first, second, next, and last. This outlined plan is designed to assist parents in putting on paper deliberate and planned steps and subsequent actions that will help them in successful child-rearing.

The purposes of this plan are to:

1) Help parents develop their thoughts and ideas about child-rearing before, during, and after the process has begun;
2) Assist parents in writing specific goals, strategies, and actions that are biblically-based, child-centered, and will promote the well-being of the child;
3) Create for parents a resource to which they can refer, monitor, and adjust for the child throughout the child-rearing process.

This plan has been prepared to cover eight main areas of child-rearing, namely, **character development, image shaping, health and wellness, parenting, home life, education, facing finances,** and **exploring the world**. Character development is the first and foundational section. It covers what parents should consider, model, and expect from their child when shaping character, conduct, and conversations. Image shaping addresses concerns parents often have about how a child looks on the outside and what needs to be done in order to shape a godly image. Health and wellness issues are explored in the third section, and it is an effort to help parents develop their ideas about maintaining good health and wellness.

Parents must address many matters while rearing children, including how they themselves will conduct their own lives and decision making. These are some of the thoughts that are examined in parenting. The home environment is the child's world and creating an environment that is appropriate for healthy growth and development is essential in child rearing. Home life challenges parents to make some thoughtful decisions about how the affairs of the home will be conducted. Education, facing finances, and exploring the world are all related to interacting with others outside of the home. Each section has subject specific concerns that allow parents to think deeply and critically about what they want for their child.

These categories emerged from reviewing the list of questions that I initially generated from my understanding of what has proven to be important over the years in my own child-rearing practices and in the lives of family and friends and their children. The plan is designed to be completed over several weeks in a workshop format, a weekend format, or an introductory version for a one-day format for whole groups or in small group studies. Discussion and reflection are necessary in order to form the foundation for what will be written and done.

Guidance, Clarity, and Wisdom

Seek God's divine direction by praying daily before you begin to think about and discuss your written responses (2 Chronicles 1:10). Pray for guidance and clarity of thought before you write your responses (Proverbs 3:5-6). Ask for wisdom from God as you plan your child's future and that of your family. There are thought provoking questions in this plan where there is no associated scripture of biblical reference just as there are issues on which the Bible is silent. In those instances, decisions and discussions should focus on principles that are in line with and consistent with understanding the nature of God's love and His will for your life.

Solomon said, "A cord of three strands is not quickly broken." Ecclesiastes 4:12. In order for a child to be successful, it takes God, the parents, and the child all focused on the plans and goals that have been developed over time with the child's best interests in mind. It takes effort on the part of families as they work to fulfill God's will for the child.

Instructions for Completing Your Plan

Think about what plans you already have for your child. What have you considered? What have you written? What's important to you? What is non-negotiable? With whom have you shared this plan? Who will hold you accountable for what is in your plan? In developing your written thoughts, you should also consider the opposite possibilities or negative effects that could occur should your focus be different.

Set aside enough time daily to pray, think about, discuss, and write clear and thoughtful responses to the questions. Think about what is pleasing to God, acceptable for you, as well as what is in the best interest of your child. There are multiple ways of correctly handling any situation. Seek God's guidance throughout this process. The key is to make sure that your planning has your child's best interests at the center and that whatever practices you choose, your actions will bring glory to God.

Complete this plan for your child using a pencil. This is a working document and is subject to change. After completing the brief Family Profile, take your time, pray and then answer the questions assigned for each day until completed. Preview the next day's questions ahead of time so that you can commit time to thinking and praying about your possible responses. The goal for answering questions daily is to begin to transform your thinking on a daily basis for child rearing. With each set of questions, you will begin to think differently and more clearly and intentionally about what you want for your child. Each section is designed to assist you in developing your plan in a different area of your child rearing. All areas are connected in that the focus is on the proper growth and development of your child. The only incorrect answers are those that are incorrect for your family. Keep this document with other important papers. You will want to refer to it at a later time. Take your time. You will never regret the time and effort that you will commit to developing this plan.

Summary

- Think about your plans and begin to pray about your responses.
- Set aside time to complete you plan. Make an appointment with yourself if necessary.
- Pray about what you will write.
- Use a pencil.
- Preview the next day's questions.
- Take your time.
- Keep your completed plan with other important papers.
- Pray for God's guidance as you work to implement your plan.

*"For I know the plans I have for you," declares the Lord, "plans to prosper you and not to harm you, plans to give you hope and a future." **Jeremiah 29:11***

Understanding Your Purpose

• •

Whenever there is a creation, the creator or designer of that creation has a specific purpose and plan for the creation. Whether it is baking a particular cake, designing clothing, creating a model object, or writing a book, the creator has a designated purpose for that object long before the object is created. And so it should be as we create children for this world. We should begin to explore purpose, our purpose for being here and then our purpose in creating others.

Do you know why you are here? What have you identified as your purpose in the world? Why did God put you here? How do you know? Answers to these questions are vital to your ability to walk in your divine calling on earth and to do what your Creator had in mind for you to do before you were born. You were created for a specific purpose to fulfill a specific need in the body of Christ. There is a purpose for your being here, and no matter what the circumstances were surrounding your birth, you were created to do something special in meeting the needs of others.

Think about who you are. What are your natural gifts? What talents have you had the opportunity to grow and cultivate over time? How do your gifts and talents come together to help you in fulfilling your purpose? Think about what you enjoy doing. How does that or could that meet a need in the world?

Your Family Profile

Complete the Family Profile prior to the first parenting session. This information will assist you in beginning to think about you and your family in meaningful and intentional ways. It will allow you to reflect on who you are and what you are capable of accomplishing as you parent. It will also help you think about and reflect on your purpose in this world and how your purpose can and will help shape that of your child's purpose.

Child's Name

_____

This name means _____ , and it was chosen because

_____ .

Child's Date of Birth _____

Address

_____City/State_____

Mother

Mother's Name _____ Age _____

High School _____College_____

Graduate School _____Major(s) _____

Hobbies

_____

Other interests/talents

_____

Career Goals: What are they?

What is your purpose in this world?

How do you know?

How have you begun to walk in your purpose?

How does your purpose meet a world need?

What is that need?

If you do not know that need, what will you do to help discover it?

Father

Father's Name _____ Age_____

High School _____

College_____

Graduate School _____Major(s)

Hobbies

_____

Other interests/talents

_____

Career Goals: What are they?

What is your purpose in this world?

How do you know?

How have you begun to walk in your purpose?

How does your purpose meet a world need?

What is that need?

If you do not know that need, what will you do to help discover it?

What resources do you need to help you find it?

Profile Summary

How are we alike and/or different? How well do we work together?

What talents and gifts do we need to examine and explore as we prepare this plan?

How do those gifts and talents affect the plan for our family?

Family Goals

"Then the Lord replied: "Write down the revelation and make it plain on tablets so that a herald may run with it. For the revelation awaits an appointed time; it speaks of the end and will not prove false. Though it linger, wait for it; it will certainly come and will not delay." Habakkuk 2:2-3

Parents should have a vision for the family as well as a mission statement that gives the family members insight and focus into what it will take in order to achieve the stated goals. Habakkuk tells us to write our vision, and when we do so, it will come to pass. It may take time, but it will happen for us if we remain in faith and continue to believe God for it.

As you respond to the questions in this section, think about vision, mission, and purpose.

1. What's your vision for your family? **Proverbs 29:18**

2. Create a mission statement for your family. (See Appendix B for an example.) On which scripture is this mission statement based?

3. Think about your closest friends and family members. List those with whom you could share this plan who would support your efforts in implementing it. Think about how and what they could contribute to your family. List those gifts.

4. List at least three individuals who will give you godly counsel about child rearing. What type of insight will each person offer your child and family?

5. What hopes do you have for your family? **Jeremiah 29:11**

6. What personal and professional sacrifices (things you give up) are you willing to make for your child's well-being and future success?

"Love the Lord your God with all your heart and with all your soul and with all your strength. These commandments that I give you today are to be upon your hearts. Impress them on your children. Talk about them when you sit at home and when you walk along the road, when you lie down and when you get up. Tie them as symbols on your hands and bind them on your foreheads. Write them on the doorframes of your houses and on your gates." **Deuteronomy 6:4-9**

SHAPING CHARACTER, CONVERSATION, AND CONDUCT

· ·

Week 1

"Love the Lord your God with all your heart and with all your soul and with all your strength. These commandments that I give you today are to be upon your hearts. Impress them on your children. Talk about them when you sit at home and when you walk along the road, when you lie down and when you get up. Tie them as symbols on your hands and bind them on your foreheads. Write them on the doorframes of your houses and on your gates." Deuteronomy 6:4-9

Parent Shaper

This passage of scripture is part of the Shema that Jewish families teach their children from birth. It is foundational to all that they do. The passage tells parents to not only love God, but to also teach their children to love God. That teaching should be a part of every aspect of the child's life, and the parents are to encourage the child in acknowledging God. This scripture is important in this plan because it is upon this passage that the rest of the plan is built. In this passage, Moses points us back to the source of our being, and to what it takes for us to be what God has created and called each of us to be in this world.

When my oldest daughter was still a toddler, my Aunt Doris gave me a piece of unsolicited, yet valuable, advice. She told me that if I got the first child in order (that is obedient and well-behaved) the others would follow suit. She said that if I trained the first one the right way, the others would follow. I took her advice because I trusted her opinion and believed that she loved me enough to tell me the right thing to do. I worked hard on training my daughter and helping her become a decent and respectable person. As it turns out, my aunt was right and her unsolicited advice was one the best pieces of advice I could have ever had.

Early in my daughter's life, I decided what values would be most important for her growth and development. I then decided that I must put forth tremendous effort in making sure that she had the appropriate life experiences that would cultivate those values. Those experiences

21

included spiritual training at home and at church, and spending time at the feet of the elderly who could and would share advice about life so that she could and would grow in the right direction.

What happened in our lives turned out to be good for my other children. My oldest daughter set the standard and the others worked hard to reach it. Shaping her character, conduct, and conversation involved daily work as a parent in teaching, correcting, and modeling the desired behavior. It was never easy, but it helped me become a better parent for my children who came after her. Shaping me helped me better plan for what I truly wanted to see in them.

This section is foundational to this plan. It is the longest section and the section with the most scriptures. Initially, I thought all sections would be comparable in length and substance, but the more I wrote about character, conduct, and conversation, the more there was to write and more questions to ask. Everything else in this plan is based on the foundation that will be laid in this section. As a parent, knowing who you want your child to become is key to making all other decisions about their upbringing. In this section, you will focus on the inner-person of your child's personality and character development as you think about shaping their thought life, their actions, and the words that they speak. Through the traits that are considered here, as a parent, you will be able to determine what you truly want for your child.

Think about your hopes and dreams for your child. What are they? How do you want your child to grow and learn? Think about your own life experiences and how those experiences can and will contribute to the hopes and dreams that you have for your child. As you complete this section and refer to the scriptures, you will be able to see what God has said through scriptures to us about how we should live and rear our children.

Spend time thinking, reflecting, and praying about your possible responses. There are no easy answers, and even in the body of Christ, there are multiple right answers to these questions. The right answer for your child is the one that works for your family, embraces your values, and does not violate biblical principles.

The following sections will allow you to list specifics about how you want your child to grow and learn. Use a pencil in order to make changes when necessary.

Day 1 – Shaping the Spirit

1. What religious and spiritual training do you want for your child? **Matthew 6:33; I Samuel 1:27-28; 2 Peter 3:18** Why?

2. Is there a particular denomination that you want for your child? If so, which one? Why? **Ephesians 4:4-7**

3. What will you do to see that it happens? **II Chronicles 1:10**

4. What do you want your child to believe about God? **I Chronicle 28:9; Psalm 121; 63:8; Ephesians 2:10**

5. What do you want your child to understand about salvation? **Romans 10:9-10,13; John 3:16; Isaiah 45:8; 2 Timothy 2:10**

6. What will you teach your child about eternity? **John 14:2-3; II Corinthians 5:1; Revelation 22:14**

Day 2

7. What do you want your child to understand about prayer, meditation, and alone time with God? **Proverbs 3:4-5, Matthew 18:18-19, 21:21, Mark 11:22-25; James 5:16; Matthew 6:5-13; I John 5:14-15; Ephesians 6:18**

8. How will you show your child how to listen to the voice of God? **John 10:4**

9. Discuss your beliefs about baptism. **Mark 16:16; Acts 1:5**

10. What scriptures are you willing to commit to memory? What are the messages you want your child to learn from these scriptures? **2 Timothy 3:16; Psalm 19:10**

11. At what age is your child accountable for her/his beliefs? _____ Discuss your reasoning for your choosing this age.

12. What are your beliefs about partaking of Holy Communion? **Luke 22:19-20; I Corinthians 11:23-26.**

13. What spiritual gifts have you identified in your child? **I Corinthians 7:7; Romans 12:4-8; I Corinthians 12; Ephesians 4:7-16; I Peter 4:10-11**

Day 3 – Shaping Character

For this reason, make every effort to add to your faith goodness; and to goodness, knowledge; and to knowledge, self-control; and to self-control, perseverance; and to perseverance, godliness; and to godliness, brotherly kindness; and to brotherly kindness, love. For if you possess these qualities in increasing measure, they will keep you from being ineffective and unproductive in your knowledge of our Lord Jesus Christ. II Peter 1:5-8

Peter gives us clear instructions as to the qualities we should aspire to having as Christians. These qualities are admirable traits that we need to embrace, model, and share with our children in the child rearing process, and as we work to grow in our knowledge and understanding of the teachings of Christ.

Think about these traits as you work through this section.

14. List the core values that shape character traits you have that you want to pass on to your child. Tell why these traits are important to you. **Proverbs 3:3; Psalm 51:10; Romans 15:13**

<u>Value</u>   <u>Importance</u>

15. How will having these values and traits help your child become a productive human being and become successful in life? **Philippians 4:8**

16. What will you do to model and promote these characteristics? **Titus 2:2-8**

17. What do you want to teach your child about life in general? **Ecclesiastes 1**

18. What do you want your child to understand about death? **I Thessalonians 4:13-18; I Corinthians 15:51-58; John 14:1-3; Psalm 30:5 and 11; Isaiah 61:3**

19. What spiritual inheritance do you want for your child?

20. What daily confessions will you make about your child? **Philippians 4:13; Psalm 119:99-100; Romans 8:37; I Corinthians 2:16; Psalm 193:14**

Day 4 – Shaping Conversations and Conduct

21. What conversations do you want to have with your child and at what age? List the topics and the appropriate age for each.

    Topic   **Age**

22. What conversations do you want your child to hear? **Matthew 12:34, 37; Proverbs 18:21; 4:24, 10: 19, 31-32; Ephesians 4:29, 5:4.**

23. List your proposed methods (talking, spanking, time out, grounding, etc.) of discipline. **Proverbs 13:24; 22:15; 23:13-14; 29:17**

24. How will your child learn self-discipline? **2 Timothy 4:5; Proverbs 1:3, 17:27; I Thessalonians 5:6**

25. What lessons do you want your child to learn about getting along with others? **Leviticus 19:18; John 15: 9, 12-13; Proverbs 17:17; Ephesians 4:32; I Peter 1:22; Romans 14:19**

26. What will you teach your child about obedience and sacrifice? **I Samuel 15:22-23; Ephesians 6:1' Colossians 3:20; I John 5:3**

Day 5

27. What do you believe about shaping your child's will? **Proverbs 22:15; I Corinthians 13:11**

28. How will these lessons be learned? Who will teach them? **II Corinthians 12:14; Ephesians 6:4**

29. What daily/weekly/monthly chores and responsibilities do you want your child to complete? Think about how those chores and responsibilities will change with age. **Colossians 3:23; Galatians 6:5**

30. What rewards do you plan to have for your child for grades, behavior, performances, etc.? **Matthew 7:11**

31. List ways that you will show praise daily to encourage your child. **Proverbs 27:2**

32. List the words you will use to show your approval of your child. **Proverbs 25:11**

Day 6

33. What will you teach your child about her/his attitude? **Matthew 5:3-11**

34. List ways that you will work to shape her/his attitude. **Philippians 2:5-11; Hebrews 4:12**

35. How will you model humility? **Philippians 2:1-4; Titus 3:2**

36. What will you teach your child about love and loving? **I Corinthians 13:1-10 and 13; Galatians 5:25; John 13:13, 34-35; I Peter 4:8; Ephesians 5:1-2; I John 4:8, 16-18**

37. What do you want your child to know about forgiveness? How will you model this for your child? **Colossians 3:13; Matthew 6:12-15; 18:21-22; Ephesians 4:32**

38. Describe how you will demonstrate justice and mercy for your child. **Psalm 11:7; Micah 6:8, Luke 6:36**

39. How will you display faith and courage on a daily basis? **Deuteronomy 31:6; Hebrews 11:1; Mark 11:22-25; Luke 17: 5-6; Matthew 21:21, 17:20; Ephesians 4:32; Colossians 3:13; Hebrews 11:1-40**

40. What do you want your child to understand about overcoming adversity? Self-doubt? **Ephesians 6:10-18; Proverbs 24:10; Isaiah 49:15-16; Deuteronomy 31:6 and 8; Joshua 1:5; Hebrews 13:5; I Peter 1:7**

Day 7

41. What will you teach your child about treating others with dignity and respect? **Mark 12:31; Proverbs 16:7**

42. How will you cultivate self-respect in your child? **I Peter 2:17**

43. What will you show your children about honesty and acting with integrity? **Proverbs 24:26; Psalm 25:21**

44. What will your teach your child about being content? **Philippians 4:11-13**

45. How will you show gratitude? To God? To your child? To other family members? **Psalm 100; Psalm 34:1; 92:1; 105:1; 106:1; Ephesians 5:20; Colossians 2:7**

46. How will you develop independent thinking and acting?

47. What will you show your child about thoughtfulness and thinking of others? **Mark 12:33**

48. How will you teach your child about accountability and being responsible for her/his actions? **Exodus 20:1-17; I Timothy 6:18-19; I Thessalonians 5:15**

49. What manners (etiquette) do you want your child to have? How will your child learn them (classes, specific training, cotillion, etc.)?

50. What will you teach your child about how to interact with adults (eye contact, saying sir and ma'am, opening doors, shaking hands)?

51. How will you model kindness, generosity, and other common courtesies? **Luke 6:38**

Summary

Shaping a child's character, conduct, and conversation is foundational to the growth and development of the child. Character speaks to who the child is when no one is looking; that is, who the child is on the inside. Conduct is what the child does and the decisions he/she makes to act in a certain way either while observed or not being observed. And conversation refers to the words that the child chooses to use. Those words can be used to give either life or death to a situation. It is those words that can also make a difference in how the child interacts with others.

Summary Activity

On your parenting plan, list 2-3 biblical goals that you want for your child in developing

Character

Conduct

Conversation.

"Be honest in your judgment and do not decide at a glance (superficially and by appearances); but judge fairly and righteously." John 7:24 (Amp)

CREATING A GODLY IMAGE

Week 2

"Be honest in your judgment and do not decide at a glance (superficially and by appearances); but judge fairly and righteously." John 7:24

Image Maker

"Everything doesn't look good on everybody," is what my mother used to tell me. That was her way of letting me know at an early age that I could not wear all of the latest styles. All styles did not fit my body type and I had to be careful about the clothes that I chose to wear if I did not want to look unattractive and be uncomfortable. It was that "mother wit" that I carried into parenting.

My children all have different sizes, body shapes, and body types. I soon realized that what looked good on one child at a certain age may not look as good on a sibling at that same age even though the clothes might fit. And so I began passing on to them the idea that they could not wear all of the styles simply because they were popular, colorful, fit them, or looked good on others. They had to learn to identify the styles that were most suitable for their bodies and to choose the clothes that were modest in appearance.

Modesty was also important in choosing clothes. Flesh was not allowed to show and neither were undergarments or items of clothing designed for personal viewing only. Each child had to learn how to cover their bodies in ways that demonstrated careful thought and consideration for self-respect and respect of others. Their clothing clearly made a statement about their self-image as well as about the image that they gave to others about how they felt about themselves. Their outer image was a reflection of the inner image that they carried with them. That understanding of self-image has remained with me and with them over the years as we continue to make clothing purchases that fit our body types.

What was probably most important to me in helping my children learn how to choose their clothing was the effort to help them understand that what they had on them was not as important as what they had in them spiritually, and that the outer garments were to be a reflection of the inner-man who was sold out to a life with Christ. I clearly understood that many people judge other people based on initial appearance and wanted them to know that while God looks at the heart, man looks at the outside. Their commitment to Christ was to be reflected in modest apparel that enhanced their appearance. John tells us that we should not judge others by how they look because it is superficial to do so. We should instead look at the righteous actions, and then make our decisions.

As you work through the questions in this section, think about the godly image that you want your child to portray to the world. Think about how you go about making clothing purchases and how you decide what your child will be allowed to wear.

In addition to body image, children also need to have a healthy self-image as described by their parents. Think about how you describe your child and her/his behavior and image to others. What words do you choose to use? Are they positive? Do they demonstrate love? How did you decide on the words that you use? Were they the same words that others used to describe you? If so, how did they make you feel?

I challenge you to begin to create for yourself a godly image of your child, and then, begin to put forth the effort to begin to create and model that image in your home for your child. You have the parental authority to make it happen. Do it for your family.

Day 1

1. List the ways that you will show love to your child on a daily basis. **I Timothy 5:8**

2. What words do you prefer to use when describing your child? **Proverbs 12:14-19; 13:2; 15:1-2; 18:20-21; 21:23**

3. What words do you want used when describing your child's behavior?

4. What friends do you want your child to have? **Proverbs 13:20; 17:17; 18:24; John 15:14; I Corinthians 15:33**

5. What relationships with other family members (i.e. siblings, extended family, grandparents, aunts, uncles) do you want your child to have?

Day 2

6. How do you want your child to be dressed (modern, traditional, mature, stylish)? **I Timothy 2:9**

7. What do you want your child to understand about choosing clothing? **I Corinthians 7:31**

8. What do you want your child to understand about their appearance in general?

9. Describe the ideal body image for your child. **Romans 12:2**

10. What life skills (cooking, cleaning, ironing, plumbing, washing, carpentry, etc.) do you want your child to have? How will these skills be taught? **Proverbs 31: 10-31; Galatians 6:5**

Therefore, I urge you, brothers, in view of God's mercy, to offer your bodies as living sacrifices, holy and pleasing to God – this is your spiritual act of worship. Do not conform any longer to the pattern of this world, but be transformed by the renewing of your mind. Then you will be able to test and approve what God's will is – his good, pleasing and perfect will. **Romans 12:1-2**

Minding Your Temple:
Health and Wellness
• •

Therefore, I urge you, brothers, in view of God's mercy, to offer your bodies as living sacrifices, holy and pleasing to God – this is your spiritual act of worship. Do not conform any longer to the pattern of this world, but be transformed by the renewing of your mind. Then you will be able to test and approve what God's will is – his good, pleasing and perfect will. Romans 12:1-2

Living Sacrifice

I didn't know he couldn't see. I knew that my youngest child always sat close to the television and constantly held the remote control. I thought it was just a power thing with him wanting to keep the remote control in his hand. The real issue was that he could not see well. They discovered that fact in kindergarten, and when I took him to the optometrist, he said my child could not see very well. I felt so badly. I thought that I had neglected my child in some way, but the truth was that I did not know he was having trouble seeing. After all, my other children who wore glasses began wearing them in third and fifth grades, and I did not wear glasses at the time either. I just had no idea he was having difficulty seeing anything, and because that was the way his vision had always been, he did not know that he was not seeing the world with the proper lens and was unable to tell me what he saw, or more importantly, what he could not see. He had never complained about his vision or his eyes.

The doctor's diagnosis was that he needed really thick lenses, but there was a way for him to have thin lenses. He also said that because of his vision, he would always need to sit at the front of the class. Otherwise, he would disengage and would not pay attention in class.

As a mother who had always tried to meet the needs of her children, I felt as if I had failed this child with regard to his vision. I wanted to apologize, but that did not make sense. I had not done anything wrong, but I felt guilty of something that I could not pinpoint. As a result of my guilt, I bought two pair of glasses for him that day. The doctor predicted he would destroy the first pair and would need a spare pair. He was right; the first pair was destroyed the first week.

The Apostle Paul tells us to present our bodies as living sacrifices to God and that we should be holy in so doing. Each of us only gets one body, and it is in that body that the spirit of God dwells. Our bodies are living temples to God and we should care for them in ways that show our reverence and respect for what God created.

This section is designed to help you think about the health and wellness of your child. Each child has differing health needs and it is up to parents to see to it that the child has what is needed in terms of health and wellness. Many of our health concerns are inherited either genetically or acquired by familial patterns of behavior that summon common illnesses. We may not have control over some of the illnesses that make their way to us, but we definitely have control over how we respond to the illness that has attached itself to us.

Think about the health and wellness issues you and your family have faced over time. Without a doubt, there are probably issues that you would have resolved differently had you had the time and opportunity to plan more effectively for an appropriate response and decision. The questions that follow will help you plan in a written format for such issues should they arise in the future.

Day 3

1. List any health concerns you may have or may anticipate having about your child.

2. What possible inherited illnesses does your family have? **Psalm 107:20**

3. How will you address these concerns?

4. What type of medical assistance will be secured for your child? *Proverbs 18:14*

5. What vaccinations will you allow your child to take? How will you explain your decision?

Day 4

6.   What foods do you want your child to enjoy? **Romans 14:14; Exodus 23:25**

7.   What foods would you rather not have your child eat? **Romans 14:14**

8.   Describe how you will design and maintain a healthy and balanced diet. **I Corinthians 6:19**

9.   What are your plans for school lunches?

10. In what physical/athletic activities will you encourage your child to engage?

11. How will you help your child manage weight?

Day 5

12. What do you want your child to understand about cleanliness?

13. What will you share with your children about personal hygiene?

14. List what is important to you about home care and household cleanliness. How will you share this with your child?

15. What do you want your child to know about sports?

16. What will you teach your child about sportsmanship?

Day 6

17. What will you teach your child about the recreational use of drugs and alcohol?

18. What will you teach your child about the proper use of prescribed medications?

19. Describe how you will use medical advice from your physician.

20. To what degree will herbs, teas, home remedies, and alternative medicines be used?

21. What home remedies will you use?

22. How will this advice interface with your belief about God's healing power? **Psalm 107:19-20; Isaiah 53:5; I Peter 2:24**

Day 7

23. What will you teach your child about human sexuality? When will you teach it? How will you teach it?

20. How do you feel about your child eating at the homes of others?

21. What will you do to maintain your mental health? **2 Timothy 1:7**

22. What will you teach your child about divine healing? **Mark 16:15-18**

Summary

Our image is only a small part of who we are, yet, society makes a much bigger deal out of our outward appearances. While our character is most important, we are often judged by how we look before we ever have an opportunity to share anything about our character. Unfortunately for many, we have to spend a lot of time focusing on how we look. In teaching our children, we should help them see and understand that while image is important, it is not the most important aspect of who they are, or of who others may be.

Summary Activity

On your parenting plan, list the three most important factors you will encourage in helping your child develop the desired image.

"By wisdom a house is built, and through understanding it is established; through knowledge its rooms are filled with rare and beautiful treasures." **Proverbs 24:3**

Cultivating Your Home Life

• •

Week 3

"Choose for yourselves this day whom you will serve…But as for me and my household, we will serve the Lord."
Joshua 24:15

"By wisdom a house is built, and through understanding it is established; through knowledge its rooms are filled with rare and beautiful treasures.
" Proverbs 24:3

Home Builder

When Marian was in first grade, her principal said that if parents would limit and monitor telephone use, there would be less confusion at school for the child and more peace at home for the family. I adopted that rule and enforced it at my home. For their entire time in school (K-12), my first four children did not have phone privileges on school nights. Their telephone privileges during any week began on Fridays after school and continued until Sunday at 5:00 p.m. If the phone rang on a week night, it was for me. This was not necessarily a biblical decision, but it was based on keeping peace in our home and on avoiding unnecessary spats and confrontations for my children at school. Maintaining a peaceful environment is a biblical principle.

Telephone privileges were given during summer months, and once they had completed college applications during their senior year of high school.

With the use of cell phones by billions of people, it has become more challenging to limit the cell phone use of my youngest child. Young people of all ages have and use cell phones. They call each other, but most of them spend hours sending and receiving text messages. This can be a major distraction and children need guidance and limits placed on their cell phone use. There are even times when it becomes necessary to confiscate the phone as well as other personal electronic devices for a period of time.

There were other rules that addressed issues such as not allowing my children to watch music videos and certain television shows and movies (those rated R). These restrictions were put in place in efforts to "guard their hearts" from images and content that my children were unable to properly process as children and teens. I later found out that there were times when they disobeyed and watched the videos anyway (they turned the channel when they heard the garage door go up). David wrote about what they were forbidden to watch on television as children in a college paper. In that paper, he talked about my rule, how they had sometimes disobeyed it, and how he had come to understand why I did not want them watching such shows on television. He acknowledged in his paper that they did not know how to handle the content of those videos and television shows.

Each of us has to establish our own guidelines for setting up a peaceful home life and maintaining the type of environment we think, feel, and believe has the potential for supporting and nurturing well-adjusted children. It is not enough to simply desire this type of home life; that desire has to have specific thoughtful actions that give real meaning to fulfilling the goal of rearing positive children.

Think about the type of home environment you want to create for your child. What will it look like? How will you create it? What tools and other resources do you need to secure in order for your ideas to become a reality for your child?

Day 1

1. Where (city, state, country) do you want to rear your child?

2. In what region of the country?

3. How much time, if any, do you want your child to spend in a foreign country?

4. What type of housing (apartment, house, condo, mobile home, family compound, reservation, duplex, etc.) do you want your child to experience?

5. What aspects of your culture and upbringing do you want reflected in your home?

Day 2

6. What guidelines (number of hours, time of day, shows, etc.) do you want in place for television viewing?

7. Who will monitor movie viewing (at home and in theaters) for your child?

8. How you will decide which television shows are appropriate for your child? **Proverbs 4:23**

9. Where will the television(s) be located in your home?

10. Will your child have her/his own bedroom? If so, how will it be organized and decorated?

11. Describe the desired bedtime routine for your child.

Day 3

12. What images/pictures do you want displayed before your child? What will these images inspire in your child?

13. What privacy policies will you have in place for your child?

14. What technology(ies) will your child use (i.e. access to the internet, computers, MP3 players, video games, email, etc)?

15. If you choose to have a computer in your home, where will it be located?

16. At what age will you give your child a cell telephone? What guidelines will you impose about cell telephone use?

17. What computer use guidelines will you implement?

Day 4

18. What additional limits will you place on your child with regard to behaviors and privileges?

19. What games do you want played in your home?

20. What toys do you want your child to have? At what age?

21. What do you want your child to learn from participating in these activities or by having these toys?

22. Who will monitor your child's play?

23. How will birthdays be celebrated?

Day 5

24. What types of music do you want heard in your home? Car?

25. What life skills do you want to teach your child?

26. Who will bring humor to your home? **Proverbs 17:22; I Thessalonians 1:6**

27. What will your child learn from you about time management? **Ecclesiastes 3:1-8**

28. What colors do you want in your home? What will these colors say about you?

Day 6

29. How will you use and conserve (wise use) energy resources (lights, water, heat, cooling, etc.) in your home?

30. What media resources (newspapers, magazines, radio news, television news) will you provide in your home?

31. Which family members will be able to offer support in child rearing?

32. How close to other family members do you want to live?

33. What pets, if any, will you have in your home? What do you think is an appropriate age for your child to have such a responsibility?

34. How will you protect your home and family? **Psalm 23 and 91**

Day 7

35. Think about the ideal home life for your child. Write a brief paragraph describing how that home life will look. Think about how you will create and maintain a peaceful and nurturing environment.

36. How will you model family prayer time?

37. Describe how you will plan family mealtime and conversation time.

38. What activities do you have in mind for spending quality time with your child?

39. List potential family outings. How will these outings help your child grow?

Summary

When we were growing up, a young classmate was teased about how the outside of his house looked. He responded, "I live on the inside and not the outside." What a profound statement to come from a child. His point was that what goes on inside of his home was more important than what happened outside of it. He was right. The home environment that parents choose to create for their children is important and will affect how the child learns to co-exist in the world. The home environment is a miniature model of the child's world and serves as the anchor for the family.

Summary Activity

On your parenting plan, complete the following activities. Think about the biblical principle that supports your thoughts.

1. Identify the people who will be influential in your home.
2. Tell where you want to live with your child.
3. List the three most important rules you will enforce daily.

"Train a child in the way he should go, and when he is old he will not turn from it."
Proverbs 22:6

Parenting Matters

• • • • • • • • • • • • • • • • • • •

Week 4

"Train a child in the way he should go, and when he is old he will not turn from it." Proverbs 22:6

Wisdom and Mother Wit

Solomon was the wisest man to ever live. He asked God for wisdom and that is what he received. Throughout Proverbs, he gives us sound instruction on many aspects of our lives. Probably the most quoted verse from that book is the one above in which direction is given to parents and caregivers of children. We are to train them in the way in which they should go, but many do not know what that way is or how to lead their children in that way.

No one grows up knowing and understanding how to parent, and even after a child has been conceived, there are still questions that parents have about child rearing. Each child is different and brings a unique set of gifts, talents, abilities, and challenges to the family. Shaping and molding those traits are the responsibilities of parents and that work is hard.

Parenting is the hardest job. It is difficult because parents are endowed with the responsibility for someone else's life. Parents must make moment-to-moment decisions that can and will have a tremendous effect on the life of the child. Those decisions are difficult because parents must use their heads and make sound choices in spite of what their hearts are feeling. Effective parenting occurs when the head and heart come together to make informed decisions that accurately and consistently meet the needs of the child. It is only through much prayer, planning, and active participation can this happen.

As a new parent many years ago, I sought guidance from The Bible, books on child rearing, and from the other mothers I knew who were able to share with me godly wisdom about what I needed to do in each situation. These women, including my mother, my aunts, and caring women at church and in the neighborhood, shared with me what they knew was important for a child to grow and develop properly. Many of these women had not read books on parenting, nor had they taken classes in child development. They had no formal training in parenting, but they had lived long enough and experienced enough of life to know what should be done and what should not be done in order to rear a child in a way that would be pleasing in the sight of God and man. They were the ones who carried the collective wisdom of the community for child rearing that was passed on from one generation to the next. It is this "mother wit" that I found useful on many occasions, for when *The Bible* seemed to be silent on certain issues, these women could readily relate a situation to a biblical principle that would offer a suggested solution. Because I knew that they loved me and my children, I always felt as if I could trust their suggestions and believed that they had our best interests at heart. As I learned more about biblical principles and what The Bible had to say about each aspect of child rearing, I grew as a parent and became more skilled at making my own decisions about rearing my children.

Unfortunately for many parents today, the type of support that I received from the "other mothers" is not as readily available. Many of us do not live near our extended families and have not yet developed the kinds of relationships with others in our communities that give us the much needed confidence to trust in their advice. Developing those relationships takes time and with the transient nature of our society, time does not always allow for long-term and meaningful relationships.

This section is very much about helping parents think about those relationships and in the absence of the development of those relationships, develop their own ideas about parenting. Much of what is in this section complements the material covered in *Shaping Character, Conduct, and Conversation*. This section seeks to help you understand just how you want to conduct what you do as a parent. These questions will help you think more deeply and clearly about your role, what you want to happen to your family, and how you want the child to interact with you and with other family members.

Think about what is involved in parenting on a daily basis. What do you know and understand about parental authority? How will you exercise that authority in the lives of your children? How important is it for you to know what to do for your child on a moment-to-moment basis?

Day 1

1. Who do you want to share in your child rearing? Tell why.

2. Who will care for your child in your absence?

3. Who will care for your child in the event of your untimely death? Catastrophic illness?

4. What provisions have you made for your child should you die before he/she reaches the age of 18?

5. When do you plan to write your will?

6. What life insurance policies do you plan to have?

Day 2

7. What do you want your child to understand about honoring you as a parent? **Exodus 20:12; Deuteronomy 5:16; Ephesians 6:2; Matthew 15:4**

8. List the child-rearing practices that you plan to enforce every day. Tell why they are important to you.

9. List the sayings, mantras, truisms that will guide your daily actions. What do they tell about you?

Day 3

10. What brings you joy as a person? As a parent? **Nehemiah 8:10; Psalm 16:11, 30:5, 126:5; Isaiah 35:10; John 16:24; Romans 14:17**

11. What are your passions?

12. What are your fears about child-rearing? How do you plan to overcome them? **I John 4:18**

13. How will you demonstrate patience? **Psalm 37:7; Ecclesiastes 7:8; Romans 12:12; James 1:4, 5:7**

14. When do you plan to take photos of your child? Your family? How often? Where will you display them? With whom will you share them?

Day 4

15. Who will have the final authority regarding decisions for your child?

16. List those who will be available in emergencies for you and your child. How will you contact them (phone, cell phone, text messaging, email, etc.)

17. List what you will read (books and authors) in order to maintain your motivation and direction as you parent your child.

18. Who will be your spiritual leader as you rear your family?

19. Describe how you will receive and use counsel from your spiritual leader. **Psalm 1**

Day 5

20. How often do you plan to communicate with your family? Your friends?

21. What are your views for overnight visits (sleepovers) at various ages?

22. How will holiday visits to families be handled? Will you travel?

3. What family heirlooms do you want your child to see? Own?

24. Are there specific material possessions that you want in your home? How will these items contribute to the healthy growth and well-being of your child? **Matthew 6:20-21**

Day 6

25. How will you convey your daily expectations to your child?

26. What will you show your child about maintaining healthy relationships?

27. What will you write about your family?

28. What limitations will you place on discussion of family matters with others?

Day 7

29. What will you teach your child about finding her/his purpose in life? **Romans 12:4-8**

30. Tell how you will model the fruit of the Spirit. *Galatians 5:22-23*

31. What place will temperance and self-control have in your lives? **Titus 2:2; I Thessalonians 5:6**

32. What legacy do you want to leave your child? Why is this important to you?

Summary

Understanding your role and responsibilities as a parent is vital for your success in child rearing. Each parent must understand the authority he/she has in the life of the child and how exercising that authority impacts the growth and development of the child. Each and every decision that a parent makes influences much in the life of a child. It is only through self-reflection and self-examination that parents begin to know and understand themselves and their roles as parents. Although parenting is never easy, it can be a well-planned process that benefits the entire family in profitable and meaningful ways.

What have you learned about your role as a parent? How has this section shaped what you will do from this day forward in parenting?

Summary Activity

On your parenting plan, identify your spiritual leader and those others who will stand beside you as you parent. Add to that section books you will read for motivation and strength and how you will seek wise counsel. Finally, list your daily expectations for your child.

"Do your best to present yourself to God as one approved, a workman who does not need to be ashamed and who correctly handles the word of truth." **2 Timothy 2:15**

Focusing on Education

• • • • • • • • • • • • • • • • • • •

Week 5

"Do your best to present yourself to God as one approved, a workman who does not need to be ashamed and who correctly handles the word of truth." 2 Timothy 2:15

"The fear of the Lord is the beginning of knowledge, but fools despise wisdom and discipline." Proverbs 1:7

Eternal Advocate

Education has always been important to my family. My grandfather, James E. Pendleton, learned to read like Frederick Douglass did using Noah Webster's <u>Blue Back Speller.</u> It was from Papa that our family began to remember stories of the importance of education. His love for learning was passed on to my mother and her siblings who in turn passed this same interest in education to me and my siblings.

That quest for knowledge demanded involvement from parents and grandparents to make sure that each child would receive the kind of education needed for success in the world. Over the years, that involvement manifested itself as advocacy on behalf of each child. For years, my mother was our advocate in school and she challenged the most difficult teachers and administrators in making sure that we had the best teachers, and when we did not have the best teachers, her consistent involvement helped teachers become better teachers. She was also the advocate who worked on our behalf when injustices were visited upon us (whether in or outside of the classroom), often leaving administrators bewildered as to how such a woman could challenge their decisions and authority in a way that often left them questioning their own professionalism, training, and decision making ability. She was the eternal advocate who could identify unfair treatment from miles away and who would not tolerate it under any circumstances. They had to do better and she demanded better for her children.

There are numerous incidents in the lives of my children that I could share about my advocating for them at school. I have had to do that for many years for my children. It is a never ending process. As parents, it is our responsibility to exercise our parental authority and to know and exercise our parental rights and responsibilities in the education processes of our children.

We must be eternal advocates on their behalf. As an advocate, certain battles will be won while others will be lost, but during the process, lessons will be learned by all about the importance of parental involvement in decision making about the education of the child. And your child will be much better for having witnessed your efforts and concern for her/his educational well-being.

Solomon and Timothy share the concern of our earthly preparation in terms of understanding the word of God. We are to prepare ourselves through time devoted to meditation and study. And so it is in the secular world as we work to present ourselves in various educational environments. We are to be prepared as though we are working unto God so that we become examples of His work in us.

The following section is designed to help you think through how you want your child to be educated. The questions are designed to make you think not only about what you want from the schools, but also about how you want to be involved in this process. In so doing, you will begin to develop ideas and plans for making sure that your child gets the kind of educational foundation needed in order to be successful in life. That is your "reasonable service." **Romans 12:1**

Day 1

1. What natural gifts have you identified in your child? How will you cultivate these gifts?

2. List the potential careers you would imagine for this child.

3. Give at least three reasons for these potential choices.

4. What talents do you want to develop in your child?

5. List what you plan to do in order to guide your child toward these choices.

6. What do you want your child to understand about education? What will you tell and model for your child so that this happens?

Day 2

7. What kind of education do you want for your child?

8. What education beyond high school (vocational school, two-year college, college, military, cosmetology school, etc.) do you want for your child?

9. What kind of college (public, private, liberal arts, two-year, etc.) do you want your child to attend?

10. What do you know about the cost of college attendance? **Luke 14:28; Proverbs 6:8; 24:27**

11. What savings plan do you have in place for paying for college? **Luke 14:28-30**

Day 3

12. In what after school activities (sports, voice/music lessons, dance, art, crafts, swimming lessons, tutoring, etc.) do you want your child to participate? Tell how you will be involved in these activities.

13. In what in-school activities (office assistant, teacher assistant, tutor, clubs, debate team, etc.) do you want your child to participate?

14. How do you envision your child spending her/his summers?

15. List important books that you want your child to hear and read at each stage of life. Tell why each book is important to you.

16. What histories (family, local, community, state, national, international, ethnic, etc.) do you want your child to know and understand? How will you share those histories?

17. What other languages do you want your child to learn? How will that happen?

18. What do you want your child to understand about healthy competition?

Day 4

19. How will you develop oral language skills in your child?

20. Tell how you plan to be involved in your child's learning.

21. What will you teach your child about the differences in doing homework and studying?

22. List the skills and talents you can offer your child's school.

23. What will you teach your child about her/his aptitude? **Psalm 119:99-100**

24. What special skills and talents do you possess that you want to see cultivated in your child?

25. What will you do to help your child learn to think critically?

Day 5

26. If your child has difficulties in school, how and where will you seek help? Who will you ask for help? **Philippians 4:13; Hebrews 12:1**

27. What special needs, if any, does your child have? How will those be addressed (parent support groups, community organizations, advocacy groups, etc.)?

28. How will you continually monitor your child's progress? How often will re-evaluation take place? Who will conduct the re-evaluation?

29. How do you feel about retention? Social promotion? Skipping a grade?

30. Tell how you will receive and use advice from teachers.

31. How will you voice your concerns to teachers?

32. How will you exercise your parental authority at your child's school?

33. What study guidelines are you willing to enforce for completing homework and preparing for tests?

34. At what age do you want your child to learn how to drive? Will driver's education classes be a part of the process?

35. What rules will you enforce related to driving? What will you model about driving?

Summary

Each child is equipped with natural gifts and talents. They also have other abilities that can be nurtured and cultivated in ways that enhance their lives. As a parent, you should know enough about your child in order to help teachers and other educators direct your child's talent and shape other abilities. It is through effective parent interactions in the education process that children are able to get the best education possible and begin to chart a course for success. Education is key and not all children are educated in the same manner. It is up to the parent to act on behalf of the child and make sure that the child's education is equitable.

Summary Activity

On your parenting plan, identify the ways in which you will help in your child's education. List the special activities (i.e. sports, dance, music lessons, etc.) that you want for your child. Write what educational opportunities you want for your child beyond high school. Tell how you plan to make sure that your child has access to those opportunities.

"Honor the Lord with your wealth, with the first fruits of all your crops; then your barns will be filled to overflowing and your vats will brim over with new wine.
Proverbs 3: 9-10.

Facing Finances

· · · · · · · · · · · · · · · · · · ·

Week 6

"Honor the Lord with your wealth, with the first fruits of all your crops; then your barns will be filled to overflowing and your vats will brim over with new wine.
Proverbs 3: 9-10.

Wise Spenders

I first heard this scripture as a little girl at St. Paul Baptist Church. Reverend Chaney, an associate minister of the gospel, would lead us in quoting this verse along with other verses about giving to God. It was in that environment that I learned that God had much to say about our money and about giving to the church.

I do not know where or how they learned to manage money, but Lauren and Jennifer have mastered it. These two young ladies have a gift for facing their finances that they did not get from their mother. They are able to think through their financial situations, give, save, and plan their spending in meaningful and profitable ways for themselves. Long ago, they decided that poverty was unattractive for them and began to work through money issues. They also had an opportunity to watch me struggle with my finances as I parented five children alone. They decided that would not be the life they would choose to have for themselves.

Unlike other young adults their ages, they have decided that eating out is not a necessity and that home cooked food is better for their skin, hair, and bodies in general. Lauren keeps gum in her purse lest she be tempted to buy fast food before mealtime. She also maintains a small weekly budget for food consumption which prompts her to sometimes buy in bulk and to look for grocery store specials before going to the store. She makes sure that she is not hungry when she goes to the store and she only goes once a week. Lastly, she cooks and takes her lunch to work at least three times a week.

Both young women only buy clothes when they are on sale, preferably marked at least 50% below the original sticker price. Because of her size, Jennifer is able to buy clothes in the children's department, the teens' department, and occasionally an item in the women's department. The items must be on sale and they are usually purchased near or at the end of the season. Like her sister, she will watch and wait for a desired item to go on sale and then will buy it with a discount coupon so that she can get the best price possible.

Facing Finances will challenge you to think about money in reference to how you as a parent choose to handle your resources. Your model of giving, saving, spending, and investing are the lessons in finances that your child will embrace or turn away from as they too become consumers. The writers of the Bible talk about money throughout and tell us where our treasures should be. Where are your treasures? What's important to you when it comes to handling your money? How is that reflected in the decisions that you make to give, save, spend, and invest? These are challenging questions, but they are ones that all parents need to discuss as we prepare our children to live outside of our homes.

Day 1

1. What do you want your child to understand about money? **Psalm 24:1, Matthew 6:24, Psalm 50:10-12, Ecclesiastes 5:10**

2. What will you do to make sure that your child learns these lessons?

3. What money use and handling skills will you model for your child? **Proverbs 21:20**

4. What ideas do you have for an allowance for your child? **Matthew 25:23; Luke 19:17**

5. What will you teach your child about credit and debt? **Psalm 37:21; Proverbs 3:28, and 22:7; Luke 12:22-32; Romans 13:7; Proverbs 22:26-27**

Day 2

6. In what areas do you struggle with money? **Proverbs 3:5-6**

7. Where do you excel with your finances?

8. What will you teach your child about God and money? **Proverbs 10:22**

Day 3

9. What will you teach about the law of sowing and reaping? **Galatians 6:7**

10. What will you share with your child about saving and investing your money? **Proverbs 21:20; Ecclesiastes 11:2**

11. What will you teach your child about tithing and giving to God? **Malachi 3:10; Luke 6:38; I Corinthians 16:1-3**. How does your use of money reflect your faith in God? What will you teach about trusting God with your money?

12. How will you plan and pay for your vacations?

Day 4

13. What inheritance do you want to leave your child? **Proverbs 13:22**

14. What will you model about caring for the poor and needy? **Acts 2:10**

15. What budgeting techniques and spending habits will you show your child?

16. What will you show your child about earning money and hard work?

Summary

Handling money can be a challenge for many parents, and modeling good financial practices can be even tougher. What makes the difference is the parent's willingness to face whatever the financial situation is and discover and implement practices and guidelines for spending, saving, giving, and investing. Our children need to see us being good stewards of our resources and facing financial matters is just one way of modeling that stewardship.

Summary Activity

List what you will teach your child about spending, saving, giving and investing their money. Think about your ideas for investing in your child. Write the three most important financial investments you want to make for your child and an estimate of what you think each will cost you. List how you will earn the resources to pay for those investments.

"*Therefore go and make disciples of all nations, baptizing them in the name of the Father and of the Son and of the Holy Spirit, and teaching them to obey everything I have commanded you. And surely I am with you always, to the very end of the age.*"
Matthew 28:19-20

Exploring the World

• • • • • • • • • • • • • • • • • • •

*"Therefore go and make disciples of all nations, baptizing them in the name
of the Father and of the Son and of the Holy Spirit, and teaching them to obey
everything I have commanded you. And surely I am with you always, to the very
end of the age."* Matthew 28:19-20

A Heart Opener

In the spring of 1977, I spent a semester in Paris, France, taking classes and learning about French language and culture. That semester offered me a cultural awakening. It was during that time that not only were my eyes opened to expecting, accepting, and respecting the differences we all bring to the world, but my heart was also opened to others.

I learned that it is important that I listen more than I speak, and that through active listening, I can learn about others in meaningful ways and begin to understand and appreciate their differences. I learned that in kingdom living, inclusion (and not exclusion) is more attuned to God's way of loving and accepting others.

When I went to Paris, I could speak French fairly well, but I was not what I would call proficient. I had a lot to learn about the subtle nuances of the language and the importance of vocal intonation in communicating with others. I was grateful for an opportunity to learn so much in a non-threatening and accepting environment.

Much of what I learned came from the people of African countries who lived in our building. Through the many interactions with them, I learned much about speaking and writing French, as well as the histories of their French-speaking countries and imperialism. I was also exposed to new foods of all flavors, colors, tastes, and textures that tantalized my taste buds.

These experiences opened my eyes, ears, and mind, but more importantly, they opened my heart to being receptive to all of the differences that others bring to an environment, and to showing God's love to everyone regardless of race, nationality, or background. This experience was truly a heart opener and it has shaped much about me as I have journeyed through the world.

Because of that experience, I have become more open to meeting new and different people. I have learned that all humans basically have the same physical, emotional, and spiritual needs, and that the only real difference in most of us is in how we go about meeting those needs. How people meet those needs is largely determined by geography, availability of resources, and access to information more than it is about anything else. That understanding remains with me and my decision making about expecting, accepting, and respecting the differences of others.

The Great Commission is mentioned throughout the New Testament. As military people would put it, those are our "marching orders" for how we are to increase the kingdom of God. We are commissioned to go to wherever people are and to share with them the good news of the resurrected Christ. It is with that single purpose in mind that we should open our hearts to receiving others.

Day 5

1. To what places do you want to travel with your child?

2. What will you teach your child about other races, cultures, and ways of living? **Mark 16:15: Matthew 13:38**

3. How will you encourage your child to give back to her/his community through service?

4. How will you model community service for your child?

5. What will you teach your child about world missions? **Psalm 96:3; Matthew 24:14, 28:19; Mark 16:15; Luke 24:47**

6. What will you model for your child about caring for the elderly, disabled, and less fortunate? **Colossians 3:12; I Peter 2:5-7**

Day 6

7. What will you teach your child about giving her/his time, talent, and treasure? **Luke 12:48, 19:13;Ephesians 6:7; I Corinthians 4:2, 6:20**

8. What political views do you plan to share with your child? What forms the foundation for these views?

9. What will you share about civic duties (voting, etc.)? **Proverbs 14:34, 24:21; Matthew 22:21; Acts 23:5; Romans 13:1; Titus 3:1**

10. What types of events (concerts, athletic events, tournaments, Olympics, cultural festivals, etc.) do you want your child to witness?

Day 7

11. What will you model about inclusion?

12. What will you teach your child about caring for the environment?

13. What "going green" strategies will you teach?

14. What societal and world issues are most important to you and your family?

15. What freedoms will you allow your child in developing her/his own ideas about the world?

16. How will you develop your child's leadership potential?

Summary

Learning to care for others helps us all understand the ways in which we need each other. While it is important that we learn to love ourselves, it is equally important that we learn to love and to show that love and acceptance to others both in and outside of our families. It is important for personal growth for children to learn how to accept those who are different, to reach out to others, and to lend a hand through service. As a parent, your example of embracing others is the image that your child will remember most.

Summary Activity

Understanding inclusion is important in accepting others and learning to serve them. Think about the service activities in which you want your child to become involved and write those on your child rearing plan. Include activities that are local, regional, national, and worldwide. Tell what you will do to support your child in becoming involved in these activities.

*"I was young and now I am old, yet I have never seen the righteous forsaken or their children begging bread. They are always generous and lend freely; their children will be blessed." **Psalm 37:25-26***

Parting Words – A Conclusion

It is said that God does not waste anything, especially pain. While child rearing has been a joy most days for me, it was not always an easy job. None of my children were intentionally planned births. The babies came and I decided prior to their births that I would do the best that I could in every area of their lives in order to make sure that they became good people. Although nothing was written to support my desire or intentions, I made every effort to make sure that they grew to be God-fearing and loving people. And although I did my best, I still faced numerous challenges along the way.

As I worked through the difficult and challenging times, I learned more about the power of prayer and the need to persevere. I knew that with God's help, I could do anything. There were times when I had to acknowledge the pain and then aim for a better decision the next time. The goal became to not repeat the same mistakes in the same way. When pain came in spite of my efforts to do the right thing, I had to investigate the source and infuse my life even more with the love of God and with what I know and understand about His nature and plan for my life. Finally, through the pain, I had to negate the thoughts that are not of God and nurture myself (with the help of family and friends) through the healing process. Going through the challenging times helped me grow, but it also provided an opportunity for me to model my belief in God and His power for my children. Simply turning to God helped in the most difficult situations.

Child rearing is the most difficult job. It involves both your head and heart and challenges parents to make critical life decisions about an individual whom they created, yet who is also equipped with a free will. It is that free will that often interferes with the best made plans.

TIPP began as a planning document that quickly grew into a living document that challenges parents to think about their child rearing practices, reflect on those practices in meaningful and constructive ways, and then to put on paper a plan for rearing each child. While the plan may be a good one and one that covers several areas of parenting, there are other areas that may need to be added. There will also always be the issue of a child's free will and how that will can and will alter any written or unwritten plan that parents may have for their child.

Free will is God's gift to us that allows us to choose good, better, and best or bad, worse, and worst from the abundance of opportunities that life sets before us. While free will helps us plan, there are often many other factors that shape the decisions that we make about any number of activities and opportunities in our lives. So although TIPP helps you plan, the contents of it are subject to change. Any written plan should allow for change, whether it is change of mind, change of circumstances, or change in opportunities. Change helps us grow and become more of the person we were intended to become from birth. Embrace change and your opportunities to grow, plan, and change even more.

Now that you have completed this process, it is my prayer that the practice of thinking about your parenting practices over a period of time has helped you think daily and more intentionally about how you choose to parent your child. Your parenting should be transformed. Intentional parenting is focused and planned with the child at the center of all decision making. TIPP is only the beginning. You have to add the love, effort, and action in order to make the things you desire a reality for you and your child.

Go in peace and God bless you and your family. To God be the glory!

Appendix A - Scriptures

Preface

Jeremiah 23:5-6 -"The days are coming," declares the LORD, when I will raise up to David [a] a righteous Branch, a King who will reign wisely and do what is just and right in the land. In his days Judah will be saved and Israel will live in safety. This is the name by which he will be called: The LORD Our Righteousness.

Isaiah 11:1-2 -A shoot will come up from the stump of Jesse; from his roots a Branch will bear fruit. [2] The Spirit of the LORD will rest on him— he Spirit of wisdom and of understanding, the Spirit of counsel and of power, the Spirit of knowledge and of the fear of the LORD –

Micah 5:2-4 -"But you, Bethlehem Ephrathah, though you are small among the clans [a] of Judah, out of you will come for me one who will be ruler over Israel, whose origins [b] are from of old, from ancient times." [3] Therefore Israel will be abandoned until the time when she who is in labor gives birth and the rest of his brothers return to join the Israelites. [4] He will stand and shepherd his flock in the strength of the LORD, in the majesty of the name of the LORD his God. And they will live securely, for then his greatness will reach to the ends of the earth.

Isaiah 7:14 -Therefore the Lord himself will give you [a] a sign: The virgin will be with child and will give birth to a son, and [b] will call him Immanuel.

Luke 1:26-37 -In the sixth month, God sent the angel Gabriel to Nazareth, a town in Galilee, [27] to a virgin pledged to be married to a man named Joseph, a descendant of David. The virgin's name was Mary. [28] The angel went to her and said, "Greetings, you who are highly favored! The Lord is with you." [29] Mary was greatly troubled at his words and wondered what kind of greeting this might be. [30] But the angel said to her, "Do not be afraid, Mary, you have found favor with God. [31] You will be with child and give birth to a son, and you are to give him the name Jesus. [32] He will be great and will be called the Son of the Most High. The Lord God will give him the throne of his father David, [33] and he will reign over the house of Jacob forever; his kingdom will never end." [34] "How will this be," Mary asked the angel, "since I am a virgin?" [35] The angel answered, "The Holy Spirit will come upon you, and the power of the Most High will overshadow you. So the holy one to be born will be called[a] the Son of God. [36] Even Elizabeth your relative is going to have a child in her old age, and she who was said to be barren is in her sixth month. [37] For nothing is impossible with God."

Matthew 1:21-23 - [21] She will give birth to a son, and you are to give him the name Jesus,[a] because he will save his people from their sins." [22] All this took place to fulfill what the Lord had said through the prophet: [23] "The virgin will be with child and will give birth to a son, and they will call him Immanuel"[b]—which means, "God with us."

Luke 1: 31-33 - You will be with child and give birth to a son, and you are to give him the name Jesus. [32] He will be great and will be called the Son of the Most High. The Lord God will give him the throne of his father David, [33] and he will reign over the house of Jacob forever; his kingdom will never end."

Philippians 2:9-11 - [9] Therefore God exalted him to the highest place and gave him the name that is above every name, [10] that at the name of Jesus every knee should bow, in heaven and on earth and under the earth,

[11]and every tongue confess that Jesus Christ is Lord, to the glory of God the Father.

Isaiah 9:6-7 -For to us a child is born, to us a son is given, and the government will be on his shoulders. And he will be called Wonderful Counselor, Mighty God, Everlasting Father, Prince of Peace. [7] Of the increase of his government and peace there will be no end. He will reign on David's throne and over his kingdom, establishing and upholding it with justice and righteousness from that time on and forever. The zeal of the LORD Almighty will accomplish this.

Isaiah 11:3-5 - and he will delight in the fear of the LORD. He will not judge by what he sees with his eyes, or decide by what he hears with his ears; [4] but with righteousness he will judge the needy, with justice he will give decisions for the poor of the earth. He will strike the earth with the rod of his mouth; with the breath of his lips he will slay the wicked. [5] Righteousness will be his belt and faithfulness the sash around his waist.

Isaiah 49:1-7 -Listen to me, you islands; hear this, you distant nations: Before I was born the LORD called me; from my birth he has made mention of my name. [2] He made my mouth like a sharpened sword, in the shadow of his hand he hid me; he made me into a polished arrow and concealed me in his quiver. [3] He said to me, "You are my servant, Israel, in whom I will display my splendor." [4] But I said, "I have labored to no purpose; I have spent my strength in vain and for nothing. Yet what is due me is in the LORD's hand, and my reward is with my God." [5] And now the LORD says—he who formed me in the womb to be his servant to bring Jacob back to him and gather Israel to himself, for I am honored in the eyes of the LORD and my God has been my strength- [6] he says: "It is too small a thing for you to be my servant to restore the tribes of Jacob and bring back those of Israel I have kept. I will also make you a light for the Gentiles, that you may bring my salvation to the ends of the earth." [7] This is what the LORD says—the Redeemer and Holy One of Israel— to him who was despised and abhorred by the nation, to the servant of rulers: "Kings will see you and rise up, princes will see and bow down, because of the LORD, who is faithful, the Holy One of Israel, who has chosen you."

Daniel 7:14 - He was given authority, glory and sovereign power; all peoples, nations and men of every language worshiped him. His dominion is an everlasting dominion that will not pass away, and his kingdom is one that will never be destroyed.

Luke 1:32-33 - He will be great and will be called the Son of the Most High. The Lord God will give him the throne of his father David, [33]and he will reign over the house of Jacob forever; his kingdom will never end."

Isaiah 42:1-4 - "Here is my servant, whom I uphold, my chosen one in whom I delight; I will put my Spirit on him and he will bring justice to the nations. He will not shout or cry out, or raise his voice in the streets. A bruised reed he will not break, and a smoldering wick he will not snuff out. In faithfulness he will bring forth justice; he will not falter or be discouraged till he establishes justice on earth. In his law the islands will put their hope."

Psalm 72:8-9, 11-17 - He will rule from sea to sea and from the River to the ends of the earth. The desert tribes will bow before him and his enemies will lick the dust. All kings will bow down to him and all nations will serve him. [12] For he will deliver the needy who cry out, the afflicted who have no one to help. [13] He will take pity on the weak and the needy and save the needy from death. [14] He will rescue them from oppression and violence, for precious is their blood in his sight. [15] Long may he live! May gold from Sheba be given him. May people ever pray for him and bless him all day long. [16] Let grain abound throughout the land; on the tops of the hills may it sway. Let its fruit flourish like Lebanon; let it thrive like the grass of the field. [17] May his name endure forever; may it continue as long as the sun.
All nations will be blessed through him, and they will call him blessed.

Isaiah 25:8 - he will swallow up death forever. The Sovereign LORD will wipe away the tears from all faces; he will remove the disgrace of his people from all the earth. The LORD has spoken.

Isaiah 53:1-12 - [1] Who has believed our message and to whom has the arm of the LORD been revealed? [2] He grew up before him like a tender shoot, and like a root out of dry ground. He had no beauty or majesty to attract us to him, nothing in his appearance that we should desire him. [3] He was despised and rejected by men, a man of sorrows, and familiar with suffering. Like one from whom men hide their faces he was despised, and we esteemed him not. [4] Surely he took up our infirmities and carried our sorrows, yet we considered him stricken by God, smitten by him, and afflicted. [5] But he was pierced for our transgressions, he was crushed for our iniquities; the punishment that brought us peace was upon him, and by his wounds we are healed. [6] We all, like sheep, have gone astray, each of us has turned to his own way; and the LORD has laid on him the iniquity of us all. [7] He was oppressed and afflicted, yet he did not open his mouth; he was led like a lamb to the slaughter, and as a sheep before her shearers is silent, so he did not open his mouth. [8] By oppression and judgment he was taken away. And who can speak of his descendants? For he was cut off from the land of the living; for the transgression of my people he was stricken. [9] He was assigned a grave with the wicked, and with the rich in his death, though he had done no violence, nor was any deceit in his mouth. [10] Yet it was the LORD's will to crush him and cause him to suffer, and though the LORD makes his life a guilt offering, he will see his offspring and prolong his days, and the will of the LORD will prosper in his hand. [11] After the suffering of his soul, he will see the light of life and be satisfied; by his knowledge my righteous servant will justify many, and he will bear their iniquities. [12] Therefore I will give him a portion among the great, and he will divide the spoils with the strong, because he poured out his life unto death, and was numbered with the transgressors. For he bore the sin of many, and made intercession for the transgressors.

Romans 12:2 – "Do not conform any longer to the pattern of this world, but be transformed by the renewing of your mind. Then you will be able to test and approve what God's will is—his good, pleasing and perfect will."

Beginning to Think and Plan

Philippians 4:8 – "Whatever is true, whatever is noble, whatever is right, whatever pure, whatever is lovely, whatever is admirable – if anything is excellent or praiseworthy – think about such things." (NIV)
Proverbs 16:3 – "Commit to the Lord whatever you do, and your plans will succeed." (NIV)
Ecclesiastes 4:12 – "A cord of three strands is not quickly broken." (NIV)

Understanding Your Purpose

Jeremiah 29:11 – "For I know the plans I have for you," declares the Lord, "plans to prosper you and not to harm you, plans to give you hope and a future." (NIV)

Habakkuk 2:2-3 – "Write down the revelation and make it plain on tablets so that a herald may run with it. For the revelation awaits an appointed time; it speaks of the end and will not prove false. Though it linger, wait for it; it will certainly come and will not delay."

Shaping, Character, Conversation, and Conduct

Matthew 6:33 – "But seek first his kingdom and his righteousness, and all these things will be given to you as well." (NIV)

I Samuel 1:27-28 – "I prayed for this child, and the Lord has granted me what I asked of him. So now I give him to the Lord. For his whole life he will be given over to the Lord." (NIV)

2 Peter 3:18 –"But grow in the grace and knowledge of our Lord and Savior Jesus Christ." (NIV)

Ephesians 4:4-6 –"Be completely humble and gentle; be patient, bearing with one another in love. Make every effort to keep the unity of the Spirit through the bond of peace. There is one body and one Spirit - just as you were called – one Lord, one faith, one baptism; one God and Father of all, who is over all and through all and in all."

II Chronicles 1:10 – "Give me wisdom and knowledge, that I may lead this people, for who is able to govern this great people of yours?"

Deuteronomy 6:4-9 – "[4] Hear, O Israel: The LORD our God, the LORD is one. [a] [5] Love the LORD your God with all your heart and with all your soul and with all your strength. [6] These commandments that I give you today are to be upon your hearts. [7] Impress them on your children. Talk about them when you sit at home and when you walk along the road, when you lie down and when you get up. [8] Tie them as symbols on your hands and bind them on your foreheads. [9] Write them on the doorframes of your houses and on your gates."

I Chronicles 28:9 - [9] "And you, my son Solomon, acknowledge the God of your father, and serve him with wholehearted devotion and with a willing mind, for the LORD searches every heart and understands every motive behind the thoughts. If you seek him, he will be found by you; but if you forsake him, he will reject you forever."

Psalm 121 – "[1] I lift up my eyes to the hills---where does my help come from? [2] My help comes from the LORD, the Maker of heaven and earth. 3 He will not let your foot slip— he who watches over you will not slumber; [4] indeed, he who watches over Israel will neither slumber nor sleep. [5] The LORD watches over you-- the LORD is your shade at your right hand; the sun will not harm you by day, nor the moon by night. [7] The LORD will keep you from all harm— he will watch over your life; [8] the LORD will watch over your coming and going both now and forevermore.

Psalm 63:8 - My soul clings to you; your right hand upholds me.

Ephesians 2:10 -For we are God's workmanship, created in Christ Jesus to do good works, which God prepared in advance for us to do.

Romans 10:9-10 and 13 - That if you confess with your mouth, "Jesus is Lord," and believe in your heart that God raised him from the dead, you will be saved. [10]For it is with your heart that you believe and are justified, and it is with your mouth that you confess and are saved. [13]for, "Everyone who calls on the name of the Lord will be saved."

John 3:16 - "For God so loved the world that he gave his one and only Son, that whoever believes in him shall not perish but have eternal life.

Isaiah 45:8 -"You heavens above, rain down righteousness; let the clouds shower it down. Let the earth open wide, let salvation spring up, let righteousness grow with it; I, the LORD, have created it.

2 Timothy 2:10 - [10]Therefore I endure everything for the sake of the elect, that they too may obtain the salvation that is in Christ Jesus, with eternal glory.

John 14:2-3 - [2]In my Father's house are many rooms; if it were not so, I would have told you. I am going there to prepare a place for you. [3]And if I go and prepare a place for you, I will come back and take you to be with me that you also may be where I am.

II Corinthians 5:1 - [1]Now we know that if the earthly tent we live in is destroyed, we have a building from God, an eternal house in heaven, not built by human hands.

Revelation 22:14 -[14]"Blessed are those who wash their robes, that they may have the right to the tree of life and may go through the gates into the city.

Proverbs 3:5-6 - [5] Trust in the LORD with all your heart and lean not on your own understanding; [6] in all your ways acknowledge him, and he will make your paths straight.

Matthew 18:18-19 - [18]"I tell you the truth, whatever you bind on earth will be bound in heaven, and whatever you loose on earth will be loosed in heaven. [19]"Again, I tell you that if two of you on earth agree about anything you ask for, it will be done for you by my Father in heaven.

Matthew 21:21 - [21]Jesus replied, "I tell you the truth, if you have faith and do not doubt, not only can you do what was done to the fig tree, but also you can say to this mountain, 'Go, throw yourself into the sea,' and it will be done.

Mark 11:22-25 - [22]"Have faith in God," Jesus answered. [23]"I tell you the truth, if anyone says to this mountain, 'Go, throw yourself into the sea,' and does not doubt in his heart but believes that what he says will happen, it will be done for him. [24]Therefore I tell you, whatever you ask for in prayer, believe that you have received it, and it will be yours. [25]And when you stand praying, if you hold anything against anyone, forgive him, so that your Father in heaven may forgive you your sins."

James 5:16 - [16]Therefore confess your sins to each other and pray for each other so that you may be healed. The prayer of a righteous man is powerful and effective.

Matthew 6:5-13 - [5]"And when you pray, do not be like the hypocrites, for they love to pray standing in the synagogues and on the street corners to be seen by men. I tell you the truth, they have received their reward in full. [6]But when you pray, go into your room, close the door and pray to your Father, who is unseen. Then your Father, who sees what is done in secret, will reward you. [7]And when you pray, do not keep on babbling like pagans, for they think they will be heard because of their many words. [8]Do not be like them, for your Father knows what you need before you ask him. [9]"This, then, is how you should pray: " 'Our Father in heaven, hallowed be your name, [10]your kingdom come, your will be done on earth as it is in heaven. [11]Give us today our daily bread. [12]Forgive us our debts, as we also have forgiven our debtors. [13]And lead us not into temptation, but deliver us from the evil one.

I John 5:14-15 - [14]This is the confidence we have in approaching God: that if we ask anything according to his will, he hears us. [15]And if we know that he hears us—whatever we ask—we know that we have what we asked of him.

Ephesians 6:18 - [18]And pray in the Spirit on all occasions with all kinds of prayers and requests. With this in mind, be alert and always keep on praying for all the saints.

John 10:4 - [4]When he has brought out all his own, he goes on ahead of them, and his sheep follow him because they know his voice.

Mark 16:16 - [16]Whoever believes and is baptized will be saved, but whoever does not believe will be condemned.
Acts 1:5 - [5]For John baptized with[a] water, but in a few days you will be baptized with the Holy Spirit."

2 Timothy 3:16 - [16]All Scripture is God-breathed and is useful for teaching, rebuking, correcting and training in righteousness…

Psalm 19:10 - They are more precious than gold, than much pure gold; they are sweeter than honey, than honey from the comb.

Luke 22:19-20 - [19]And he took bread, gave thanks and broke it, and gave it to them, saying, "This is my body given for you; do this in remembrance of me." [20]In the same way, after the supper he took the cup, saying, "This cup is the new covenant in my blood, which is poured out for you.

I Corinthians 11:23-26 - For I received from the Lord what I also passed on to you: The Lord Jesus, on the night he was betrayed, took bread, [24]and when he had given thanks, he broke it and said, "This is my body, which is for you; do this in remembrance of me." [25]In the same way, after supper he took the cup, saying, "This cup is the new covenant in my blood; do this, whenever you drink it, in remembrance of me." [26]For whenever you eat this bread and drink this cup, you proclaim the Lord's death until he comes.

I Corinthians 7:7 - I wish that all men were as I am. But each man has his own gift from God; one has this gift, another has that.

II Peter 1:5-8 - [5]For this very reason, make every effort to add to your faith goodness; and to goodness, knowledge; [6]and to knowledge, self-control; and to self-control, perseverance; and to perseverance, godliness; [7]and to godliness, brotherly kindness; and to brotherly kindness, love. [8]For if you possess these qualities in increasing measure, they will keep you from being ineffective and unproductive in your knowledge of our Lord Jesus Christ.

Proverbs 3:3 - Let love and faithfulness never leave you; bind them around your neck, write them on the tablet of your heart.

Psalm 51:10 - Create in me a pure heart, O God, and renew a steadfast spirit within me.

Romans 15:13 - May the God of hope fill you with all joy and peace as you trust in him, so that you may overflow with hope by the power of the Holy Spirit.

Philippians 4:8 - Finally, brothers, whatever is true, whatever is noble, whatever is right, whatever is pure, whatever is lovely, whatever is admirable—if anything is excellent or praiseworthy—think about such things.

Titus 2:2-8 - [2]Teach the older men to be temperate, worthy of respect, self-controlled, and sound in faith, in love and in endurance. [3]Likewise, teach the older women to be reverent in the way they live, not to be slanderers or addicted to much wine, but to teach what is good. [4]Then they can train the younger women to love their husbands and children, [5]to be self-controlled and pure, to be busy at home, to be kind, and to be subject to their husbands, so that no one will malign the word of God. [6]Similarly, encourage the young men to be self-controlled. [7]In everything set them an example by doing what is good. In your teaching show integrity, seriousness [8]and soundness of speech that cannot be condemned, so that those who oppose you may be ashamed because they have nothing bad to say about us.

I Thessalonians 4:13-18 - [13]Brothers, we do not want you to be ignorant about those who fall asleep, or to grieve like the rest of men, who have no hope. [14]We believe that Jesus died and rose again and so we believe that God will bring with Jesus those who have fallen asleep in him. [15]According to the Lord's own word, we tell you that we who are still alive, who are left till the coming of the Lord, will certainly not precede those who have fallen asleep. [16]For the Lord himself will come down from heaven, with a loud command, with the voice of the archangel and with the trumpet call of God, and the dead in Christ will rise first. [17]After that, we who are still alive and are left will be caught up together with them in the clouds to meet the Lord in the air. And so we will be with the Lord forever. [18]Therefore encourage each other with these words.

I Corinthians 15:51-58 - [51]Listen, I tell you a mystery: We will not all sleep, but we will all be changed— [52]in a flash, in the twinkling of an eye, at the last trumpet. For the trumpet will sound, the dead will be raised imperishable, and we will be changed. [53]For the perishable must clothe itself with the imperishable, and the mortal with immortality. [54]When the perishable has been clothed with the imperishable, and the mortal with immortality, then the saying that is written will come true: "Death has been swallowed up in victory." [55]"Where, O death, is your victory? Where, O death, is your sting?"[b] [56]The sting of death is sin, and the power of sin is the law. [57]But thanks be to God! He gives us the victory through our Lord Jesus Christ. [58]Therefore, my dear brothers, stand firm. Let nothing move you. Always give yourselves fully to the work of the Lord, because you know that your labor in the Lord is not in vain.

John 14:1-3 - [1]"Do not let your hearts be troubled. Trust in God[a]; trust also in me. [2]In my Father's house are many rooms; if it were not so, I would have told you. I am going there to prepare a place for you. [3]And if I go and prepare a place for you, I will come back and take you to be with me that you also may be where I am.

Psalm 30:5 and 11 - [5] For his anger lasts only a moment, but his favor lasts a lifetime;
weeping may remain for a night, but rejoicing comes in the morning. [11] You turned my wailing into dancing; you removed my sackcloth and clothed me with joy…

Isaiah 61:3 - [3] and provide for those who grieve in Zion— to bestow on them a crown of beauty instead of ashes, the oil of gladness instead of mourning, and a garment of praise instead of a spirit of despair. They will be called oaks of righteousness, a planting of the LORD for the display of his splendor.

Philippians 4:13 - I can do everything through him who gives me strength.

Psalm 119: 99-100 - [99] I have more insight than all my teachers, for I meditate on your statutes. [100] I have more understanding than the elders, for I obey your precepts.

Romans 8:37 - [37]No, in all these things we are more than conquerors through him who loved us.

II Corinthians 2:16 - [16]"For who has known the mind of the Lord that he may instruct him?" But we have the mind of Christ.

Psalm 139:14 - [14] I praise you because I am fearfully and wonderfully made; your works are wonderful, I know that full well.

Matthew 12:34 and 37 - You brood of vipers, how can you who are evil say anything good? For out of the overflow of the heart the mouth speaks. [37]For by your words you will be acquitted, and by your words you will be condemned."

Proverbs 18:21 - [21] The tongue has the power of life and death, and those who love it will eat its fruit.

Proverbs 4:24 - [24] Put away perversity from your mouth; keep corrupt talk far from your lips.

Proverbs 10:19 - [19] When words are many, sin is not absent, but he who holds his tongue is wise., **31-32** - [31] The mouth of the righteous brings forth wisdom, but a perverse tongue will be cut out. [32] The lips of the righteous know what is fitting, but the mouth of the wicked only what is perverse. **17:27** - [27] A man of knowledge uses words with restraint, and a man of understanding is even-tempered.

Ephesians 4:29 - [29]Do not let any unwholesome talk come out of your mouths, but only what is helpful for building others up according to their needs, that it may benefit those who listen.

Ephesians 5:4 - [4]Nor should there be obscenity, foolish talk or coarse joking, which are out of place, but rather thanksgiving.

Proverbs 22: 15 - [15] Folly is bound up in the heart of a child, but the rod of discipline will drive it far from him.

Proverbs 13:24 - [24] He who spares the rod hates his son, but he who loves him is careful to discipline him.

Proverbs 23:13-14 - [13] Do not withhold discipline from a child; if you punish him with the rod, he will not die. [14] Punish him with the rod and save his soul from death

Proverbs 29:17 - [17] Discipline your son, and he will give you peace; he will bring delight to your soul.

2 Timothy 4:5 - [5]But you, keep your head in all situations, endure hardship, do the work of an evangelist, discharge all the duties of your ministry.

I Thessalonians 5:6 - [6]So then, let us not be like others, who are asleep, but let us be alert and self-controlled.

Proverbs 1:3 - [3] for acquiring a disciplined and prudent life, doing what is right and just and fair;

Leviticus 19:18 - [18] " 'Do not seek revenge or bear a grudge against one of your people, but love your neighbor as yourself. I am the LORD.

John 15:9, 12-13 - [9]"As the Father has loved me, so have I loved you. Now remain in my love. [12]My command is this: Love each other as I have loved you. [13]Greater love has no one than this, that he lay down his life for his friends.

Proverbs 17:17 - [17] A friend loves at all times, and a brother is born for adversity.

Ephesians 4:32 - [32]Be kind and compassionate to one another, forgiving each other, just as in Christ God forgave you.

I Peter 1:22 - [22]Now that you have purified yourselves by obeying the truth so that you have sincere love for your brothers, love one another deeply, from the heart.

Romans 14:19 - [19]Let us therefore make every effort to do what leads to peace and to mutual edification.

I Samuel 15:22-23 - [22] But Samuel replied: "Does the LORD delight in burnt offerings and sacrifices as much as in obeying the voice of the LORD ? To obey is better than sacrifice, and to heed is better than the fat of rams. [23] For rebellion is like the sin of divination, and arrogance like the evil of idolatry. Because you have rejected the word of the LORD, he has rejected you as king."

Ephesians 6:1 - [1]Children, obey your parents in the Lord, for this is right.

Colossians 3:20 - [20]Children, obey your parents in everything, for this pleases the Lord.

I John 5:3 - [3]This is love for God: to obey his commands. And his commands are not burdensome…

Proverbs 22:15 - [15] Folly is bound up in the heart of a child, but the rod of discipline will drive it far from him.

I Corinthians 13:11 - [11]When I was a child, I talked like a child, I thought like a child, I reasoned like a child. When I became a man, I put childish ways behind me.

II Corinthians 12:14 - [14]Now I am ready to visit you for the third time, and I will not be a burden to you, because what I want is not your possessions but you. After all, children should not have to save up for their parents, but parents for their children.

Ephesians 6:4 - [4]Fathers, do not exasperate your children; instead, bring them up in the training and instruction of the Lord.

Colossians 3:23 - [23]Whatever you do, work at it with all your heart, as working for the Lord, not for men…

Galatians 6:5 - [5]for each one should carry his own load.

Matthew 7:11 - [11]If you, then, though you are evil, know how to give good gifts to your children, how much more will your Father in heaven give good gifts to those who ask him!

Proverbs 27:2 - [2] Let another praise you, and not your own mouth; someone else, and not your own lips.

Proverbs 25:11 - [11] A word aptly spoken is like apples of gold in settings of silver.

Matthews 5:3-11 - [3]"Blessed are the poor in spirit, for theirs is the kingdom of heaven. [4]Blessed are those who mourn, for they will be comforted. [5]Blessed are the meek, for they will inherit the earth.

[6]Blessed are those who hunger and thirst for righteousness, for they will be filled. [7]Blessed are the merciful, for they will be shown mercy. [8]Blessed are the pure in heart, for they will see God. [9]Blessed are the peacemakers, for they will be called sons of God. [10]Blessed are those who are persecuted because of righteousness, for theirs is the kingdom of heaven. [11]"Blessed are you when people insult you, persecute you and falsely say all kinds of evil against you because of me.

Philippians 2:5-11 - [5]Your attitude should be the same as that of Christ Jesus: [6]Who, being in very nature God, did not consider equality with God something to be grasped, [7]but made himself nothing, taking the very nature of a servant, being made in human likeness. [8]And being found in appearance as a man, he humbled himself and became obedient to death— even death on a cross! [9]Therefore God exalted him to the highest place and gave him the name that is above every name, [10]that at the name of Jesus every knee should bow, in heaven and on earth and under the earth, [11]and every tongue confess that Jesus Christ is Lord, to the glory of God the Father.

Hebrews 4:12 - [12]For the word of God is living and active. Sharper than any double-edged sword, it penetrates even to dividing soul and spirit, joints and marrow; it judges the thoughts and attitudes of the heart.

Philippians 2:1-4 - [1]If you have any encouragement from being united with Christ, if any comfort from his love, if any fellowship with the Spirit, if any tenderness and compassion, [2]then make my joy complete by being like-minded, having the same love, being one in spirit and purpose. [3]Do nothing out of selfish ambition or vain conceit, but in humility consider others better than yourselves. [4]Each of you should look not only to your own interests, but also to the interests of others.

Titus 3:2 - [2]to slander no one, to be peaceable and considerate, and to show true humility toward all men.

I Corinthians 13:1-10 and 13 - [1]If I speak in the tongues of men and of angels, but have not love, I am only a resounding gong or a clanging cymbal. [2]If I have the gift of prophecy and can fathom all mysteries and all knowledge, and if I have a faith that can move mountains, but have not love, I am nothing. [3]If I give all I possess to the poor and surrender my body to the flames, but have not love, I gain nothing. [4]Love is patient, love is kind. It does not envy, it does not boast, it is not proud. [5]It is not rude, it is not self-seeking, it is not easily angered, it keeps no record of wrongs. [6]Love does not delight in evil but rejoices with the truth. [7]It always protects, always trusts, always hopes, always perseveres. [8]Love never fails. But where there are prophecies, they will cease; where there are tongues, they will be stilled; where there is knowledge, it will pass away. [9]For we know in part and we prophesy in part, [10]but when perfection comes, the imperfect disappears. [13]And now these three remain: faith, hope and love. But the greatest of these is love.

John 13:13 - [13]"You call me 'Teacher' and 'Lord,' and rightly so, for that is what I am.
34-35 - [34]"A new command I give you: Love one another. As I have loved you, so you must love one another. [35]By this all men will know that you are my disciples, if you love one another."

I Peter 4:8 - [8]Above all, love each other deeply, because love covers over a multitude of sins.

Ephesians 5:1-2 - [1]Be imitators of God, therefore, as dearly loved children [2]and live a life of love, just as Christ loved us and gave himself up for us as a fragrant offering and sacrifice to God.

I John 4:8- [8]Whoever does not love does not know God, because God is love.
16-18 - [16]And so we know and rely on the love God has for us. God is love. Whoever lives in love lives in God, and God in him. [17]In this way, love is made complete among us so that we will have confidence on the day of judgment, because in this world we are like him. [18]There is no fear in love. But perfect love drives out fear, because fear has to do with punishment. The one who fears is not made perfect in love.

Galatians 5:25 - [25]Since we live by the Spirit, let us keep in step with the Spirit.

Colossians 3:13 - [13]Bear with each other and forgive whatever grievances you may have against one another. Forgive as the Lord forgave you.

Matthew 6:12-15 - [12]Forgive us our debts, as we also have forgiven our debtors. [13]And lead us not into temptation, but deliver us from the evil one. [14]For if you forgive men when they sin against you, your heavenly Father will also forgive you. [15]But if you do not forgive men their sins, your Father will not forgive your sins.

Matthew 18:21-22 - [21]Then Peter came to Jesus and asked, "Lord, how many times shall I forgive my brother when he sins against me? Up to seven times?" [22]Jesus answered, "I tell you, not seven times, but seventy-seven times.

Ephesians 4:32 - [32]Be kind and compassionate to one another, forgiving each other, just as in Christ God forgave you.

Psalm 11:7 - [7] For the LORD is righteous, he loves justice; upright men will see his face.

Micah 6:8 - [8] He has showed you, O man, what is good. And what does the LORD require of you? To act justly and to love mercy and to walk humbly with your God.

Luke 6:36 - [36]Be merciful, just as your Father is merciful.

Hebrews 11:1 - [1]Now faith is the substance of things hoped for, the evidence of things not seen. (KJV)

Mark 11:22-25 - [22]And Jesus answering saith unto them, Have faith in God. [23]For verily I say unto you, That whosoever shall say unto this mountain, Be thou removed, and be thou cast into the sea; and shall not doubt in his heart, but shall believe that those things which he saith shall come to pass; he shall have whatsoever he saith. [24]Therefore I say unto you, What things soever ye desire, when ye pray, believe that ye receive them, and ye shall have them. [25]And when ye stand praying, forgive, if ye have ought against any: that your Father also which is in heaven may forgive you your trespasses.

Matthew 21:21 - [21]Jesus answered and said unto them, Verily I say unto you, If ye have faith, and doubt not, ye shall not only do this which is done to the fig tree, but also if ye shall say unto this mountain, Be thou removed, and be thou cast into the sea; it shall be done.

Matthew 17:20 - [20]He replied, "Because you have so little faith. I tell you the truth, if you have faith as small as a mustard seed, you can say to this mountain, 'Move from here to there' and it will move. Nothing will be impossible for you."

Ephesians 4:32 - [32]Be kind and compassionate to one another, forgiving each other, just as in Christ God forgave you.

Colossians 3:13 - [13]Bear with each other and forgive whatever grievances you may have against one another. Forgive as the Lord forgave you.

Luke 17:5-6 - [5]The apostles said to the Lord, "Increase our faith!" [6]He replied, "If you have faith as small as a mustard seed, you can say to this mulberry tree, 'Be uprooted and planted in the sea,' and it will obey you.

Hebrews 11:1 - [1]Now faith is being sure of what we hope for and certain of what we do not see.

Deuteronomy 31:6 - Be strong and courageous. Do not be afraid or terrified because of them, for the LORD your God goes with you; he will never leave you nor forsake you."

Ephesians 6:10-18 - [10]Finally, be strong in the Lord and in his mighty power. [11]Put on the full armor of God so that you can take your stand against the devil's schemes. [12]For our struggle is not against flesh and blood, but against the rulers, against the authorities, against the powers of this dark world and against the spiritual forces of evil in the heavenly realms. [13]Therefore put on the full armor of God, so that when the day of evil comes, you may be able to stand your ground, and after you have done everything, to stand. [14]Stand firm then, with the belt of truth buckled around your waist, with the breastplate of righteousness in place, [15]and with your feet fitted with the readiness that comes from the gospel of peace. [16]In addition to all this, take up the shield of faith, with which you can extinguish all the flaming arrows of the evil one. [17]Take the helmet of salvation and the sword of the Spirit, which is the word of God. [18]And pray in the Spirit on all occasions with all kinds of prayers and requests. With this in mind, be alert and always keep on praying for all the saints.

Proverbs 24:10 - [10] If you falter in times of trouble, how small is your strength!

Mark 12:31 - The second is this: 'Love your neighbor as yourself.' There is no commandment greater than these."

Proverbs 16:7 - [7] When a man's ways are pleasing to the LORD, he makes even his enemies live at peace with him.

Proverbs 24:26 - [26] An honest answer is like a kiss on the lips.

Isaiah 49:15-16 - [15] "Can a mother forget the baby at her breast and have no compassion on the child she has borne? Though she may forget, I will not forget you! [16] See, I have engraved you on the palms of my hands; your walls are ever before me.

Deuteronomy 31:6 and 8 [6] Be strong and courageous. Do not be afraid or terrified because of them, for the LORD your God goes with you; he will never leave you nor forsake you." [8] The LORD himself goes before you and will be with you; he will never leave you nor forsake you. Do not be afraid; do not be discouraged."

Joshua 1:5 - ⁵ No one will be able to stand up against you all the days of your life. As I was with Moses, so I will be with you; I will never leave you nor forsake you.

Hebrews 13:5 - ⁵Keep your lives free from the love of money and be content with what you have, because God has said, "Never will I leave you; never will I forsake you."

I Peter 1:7 - ⁷These have come so that your faith—of greater worth than gold, which perishes even though refined by fire—may be proved genuine and may result in praise, glory and honor when Jesus Christ is revealed.

I Peter 2:17 - ¹⁷Show proper respect to everyone: Love the brotherhood of believers, fear God, honor the king.

Psalm 25:21 - ²¹ May integrity and uprightness protect me, because my hope is in you.

Philippians 4:11-13 - ¹¹I am not saying this because I am in need, for I have learned to be content whatever the circumstances. ¹²I know what it is to be in need, and I know what it is to have plenty. I have learned the secret of being content in any and every situation, whether well fed or hungry, whether living in plenty or in want. ¹³I can do everything through him who gives me strength.

Psalm 100 - ¹ Shout for joy to the LORD, all the earth. ² Worship the LORD with gladness; come before him with joyful songs. ³ Know that the LORD is God. It is he who made us, and we are his; we are his people, the sheep of his pasture. ⁴ Enter his gates with thanksgiving and his courts with praise; give thanks to him and praise his name. ⁵ For the LORD is good and his love endures forever; his faithfulness continues through all generations.

Psalm 34:1 - I will extol the LORD at all times; his praise will always be on my lips.

Psalm 92:1 - It is good to praise the LORD and make music to your name, O Most High,

Psalm 105:1 - Give thanks to the LORD, call on his name; make known among the nations what he has done.

Psalm 106:1 - Praise the LORD. Give thanks to the LORD, for he is good; his love endures forever.

Ephesians 5:20 - ²⁰always giving thanks to God the Father for everything, in the name of our Lord Jesus Christ.

Colossians 2:7 - ⁷rooted and built up in him, strengthened in the faith as you were taught, and overflowing with thankfulness.

Mark 12:33 - ³³To love him with all your heart, with all your understanding and with all your strength, and to love your neighbor as yourself is more important than all burnt offerings and sacrifices."

Exodus 20:1-17 - ¹ And God spoke all these words: ² "I am the LORD your God, who brought you out of Egypt, out of the land of slavery. ³ "You shall have no other gods before me. ⁴ "You shall not make for yourself an idol in the form of anything in heaven above or on the earth beneath or in the waters below. ⁵ You shall not bow down to them or worship them; for I, the LORD your God, am a jealous God, punishing the children for the sin of the fathers to the third and fourth generation of those who hate me, ⁶ but showing love to a thousand {generations} of those who love me and keep my commandments. ⁷ "You shall not misuse the name of the LORD your God, for the LORD will not hold anyone guiltless who misuses his name. ⁸ "Remember the Sabbath day by keeping it holy. ⁹ Six days you shall labor and do all your work, ¹⁰ but the seventh day is a Sabbath to the LORD your God. On it you shall not do any work, neither you, nor your son or daughter, nor your manservant or maidservant, nor your animals, nor the alien within your gates. ¹¹ For in six days the LORD made the heavens and the earth, the sea, and all that is in them, but he rested on the seventh day. Therefore the LORD blessed the Sabbath day and made it holy. ¹² "Honor your father and your mother, so that you may live long in the land the LORD your God is giving you. ¹³ "You shall not murder. ¹⁴ "You shall not commit adultery. ¹⁵ "You shall not steal. ¹⁶ "You shall not give false testimony against your neighbor. ¹⁷ "You shall not covet your neighbor's house. You shall not covet your neighbor's wife, or his manservant or maidservant, his ox or donkey, or anything that belongs to your neighbor."

Luke 6:38 - ³⁸Give, and it will be given to you. A good measure, pressed down, shaken together and running over, will be poured into your lap. For with the measure you use, it will be measured to you."

I Timothy 6:18-19 - Command them to do good, to be rich in good deeds, and to be generous and willing to share.

[19]In this way they will lay up treasure for themselves as a firm foundation for the coming age, so that they may take hold of the life that is truly life.

I Thessalonians 5:15 - [15]Make sure that nobody pays back wrong for wrong, but always try to be kind to each other and to everyone else.

Creating a Godly Image

John 7:24 - [24]Stop judging by mere appearances, and make a right judgment."

I Timothy 5:8 - [8]If anyone does not provide for his relatives, and especially for his immediate family, he has denied the faith and is worse than an unbeliever.

Proverbs 12:14-19 - [14] From the fruit of his lips a man is filled with good things as surely as the work of his hands rewards him. [15] The way of a fool seems right to him, but a wise man listens to advice. [16] A fool shows his annoyance at once, but a prudent man overlooks an insult. [17] A truthful witness gives honest testimony, but a false witness tells lies. [18] Reckless words pierce like a sword, but the tongue of the wise brings healing. [19] Truthful lips endure forever, but a lying tongue lasts only a moment.

Proverbs 13:2 - [2] From the fruit of his lips a man enjoys good things, but the unfaithful have a craving for violence.

Proverbs 15:1-2 - [1] A gentle answer turns away wrath, but a harsh word stirs up anger. [2] The tongue of the wise commends knowledge, but the mouth of the fool gushes folly.

Proverbs 18:20-23 - [20] From the fruit of his mouth a man's stomach is filled; with the harvest from his lips he is satisfied. [21] The tongue has the power of life and death, and those who love it will eat its fruit. [22] He who finds a wife finds what is good and receives favor from the LORD. [23] A poor man pleads for mercy, but a rich man answers harshly.

Proverbs 13:20 - [20] He who walks with the wise grows wise, but a companion of fools suffers harm.

Proverbs 17:17 - [17] A friend loves at all times, and a brother is born for adversity.

Proverbs 18:24 - [24] A man of many companions may come to ruin, but there is a friend who sticks closer than a brother.

John 15:14 - [14]You are my friends if you do what I command.

I Corinthians 15:33 - [33]Do not be misled: "Bad company corrupts good character."

I Timothy 2:9 - [9]I also want women to dress modestly, with decency and propriety, not with braided hair or gold or pearls or expensive clothes…

I Corinthians 7:31 - [31]those who use the things of the world, as if not engrossed in them. For this world in its present form is passing away.

Romans 12:2 - [2]Do not conform any longer to the pattern of this world, but be transformed by the renewing of your mind. Then you will be able to test and approve what God's will is—his good, pleasing and perfect will.

Proverbs 31:10-31 – The virtuous woman
Galatians 6:5 - [5]for each one should carry his own load.

Minding Your Temple

I Corinthians 6:19 - [19]Do you not know that your body is a temple of the Holy Spirit, who is in you, whom you have received from God? You are not your own;

Romans 12:1-2 - [1]Therefore, I urge you, brothers, in view of God's mercy, to offer your bodies as living sacrifices, holy and pleasing to God—this is your spiritual[a] act of worship. [2]Do not conform any longer to the pattern of this world, but be transformed by the renewing of your mind. Then you will be able to test and approve what God's will is—his good, pleasing and perfect will.

Psalm 107:20 - [20] He sent forth his word and healed them; he rescued them from the grave.

Isaiah 53:5 - [5] But he was pierced for our transgressions, he was crushed for our iniquities; the punishment that brought us peace was upon him, and by his wounds we are healed.

I Peter 2:24 - [24]He himself bore our sins in his body on the tree, so that we might die to sins and live for righteousness; by his wounds you have been healed.

Proverbs 18:14 - [14] A man's spirit sustains him in sickness, but a crushed spirit who can bear?

Romans 14:14 - [14]As one who is in the Lord Jesus, I am fully convinced that no food is unclean in itself. But if anyone regards something as unclean, then for him it is unclean.

Exodus 23:25 - [25] Worship the LORD your God, and his blessing will be on your food and water. I will take away sickness from among you…

2 Timothy 1:7 - [7]For God did not give us a spirit of timidity, but a spirit of power, of love and of self-discipline.

Mark 16:15-18 - [15]He said to them, "Go into all the world and preach the good news to all creation. [16]Whoever believes and is baptized will be saved, but whoever does not believe will be condemned. [17]And these signs will accompany those who believe: In my name they will drive out demons; they will speak in new tongues; [18]they will pick up snakes with their hands; and when they drink deadly poison, it will not hurt them at all; they will place their hands on sick people, and they will get well."

Cultivating Your Home Life

Proverbs 31:10-31 – The virtuous woman

Proverbs 24:3 - [3] By wisdom a house is built, and through understanding it is established;

Proverbs 4:23 - [23] Above all else, guard your heart, for it is the wellspring of life.

Proverbs 17:22 - [22] A cheerful heart is good medicine, but a crushed spirit dries up the bones.

Proverbs 15:13 - [13] A happy heart makes the face cheerful, but heartache crushes the spirit.

I Thessalonians 1:6 - [6]You became imitators of us and of the Lord; in spite of severe suffering, you welcomed the message with the joy given by the Holy Spirit.

Ecclesiastes 3:1-8 - [1] There is a time for everything, and a season for every activity under heaven: [2] a time to be born and a time to die, a time to plant and a time to uproot, [3] a time to kill and a time to heal, a time to tear down and a time to build, [4] a time to weep and a time to laugh, a time to mourn and a time to dance, [5] a time to scatter stones and a time to gather them, a time to embrace and a time to refrain, [6] a time to search and a time to give up, a time to keep and a time to throw away, [7] a time to tear and a time to mend, a time to be silent and a time to speak, [8] a time to love and a time to hate, a time for war and a time for peace.

Proverbs 4:23 - [23] Above all else, guard your heart, for it is the wellspring of life.

Psalm 23 – The Lord is my shepherd.

Psalm 91 – The secret place of the most high.

Parenting Matters

Proverbs 22:6 - [6] Train a child in the way he should go, and when he is old he will not turn from it.

Exodus 20:12 - [12] "Honor your father and your mother, so that you may live long in the land the LORD your God is giving you.
Deuteronomy 5:16 - [16] "Honor your father and your mother, as the LORD your God has commanded you, so that you may live long and that it may go well with you in the land the LORD your God is giving you.

Ephesians 6:2 - [2]"Honor your father and mother"—which is the first commandment with a promise—

Matthew 15:4 - [4]For God said, 'Honor your father and mother'[a] and 'Anyone who curses his father or mother must be put to death.'

Nehemiah 8:10 - [10] Nehemiah said, "Go and enjoy choice food and sweet drinks, and send some to those who have nothing prepared. This day is sacred to our Lord. Do not grieve, for the joy of the LORD is your strength."

Psalm 16:11 - [11] You have made known to me the path of life; you will fill me with joy in your presence, with eternal pleasures at your right hand., **30:5** - [5] For his anger lasts only a moment, but his favor lasts a lifetime; weeping may remain for a night, but rejoicing comes in the morning., **126:5** - [5] Those who sow in tears will reap with songs of joy.

Isaiah 35:10 - [10] and the ransomed of the LORD will return. They will enter Zion with singing; everlasting joy will crown their heads. Gladness and joy will overtake them, and sorrow and sighing will flee away.

John 16:24 - [24]Until now you have not asked for anything in my name. Ask and you will receive, and your joy will be complete.

Romans 14:17- [17]For the kingdom of God is not a matter of eating and drinking, but of righteousness, peace and joy in the Holy Spirit…

I John 4:18 - [18]There is no fear in love. But perfect love drives out fear, because fear has to do with punishment. The one who fears is not made perfect in love.

Psalm 37:7 - [7] Be still before the LORD and wait patiently for him; do not fret when men succeed in their ways, when they carry out their wicked schemes.

Ecclesiastes 7:8 - [8] The end of a matter is better than its beginning, and patience is better than pride.

Romans 12:12 - [12]Be joyful in hope, patient in affliction, faithful in prayer.

James 1:4 - [4]Perseverance must finish its work so that you may be mature and complete, not lacking anything., **5:7** - [7]Be patient, then, brothers, until the Lord's coming. See how the farmer waits for the land to yield its valuable crop and how patient he is for the autumn and spring rains.

Psalm I - All

Matthew 6:20-21 - [20]But store up for yourselves treasures in heaven, where moth and rust do not destroy, and where thieves do not break in and steal. [21]For where your treasure is, there your heart will be also. [20]But store up for yourselves treasures in heaven, where moth and rust do not destroy, and where thieves do not break in and steal. [21]For where your treasure is, there your heart will be also.

Galatians 5:22-23 - [22]But the fruit of the Spirit is love, joy, peace, patience, kindness, goodness, faithfulness, [23]gentleness and self-control. Against such things there is no law.

Titus 2:2- [2]Teach the older men to be temperate, worthy of respect, self-controlled, and sound in faith, in love and in endurance.

I Thessalonians 5:6 - [6]So then, let us not be like others, who are asleep, but let us be alert and self-controlled.

Focusing on Education

Romans 12:11 - [11]Never be lacking in zeal, but keep your spiritual fervor, serving the Lord.

Luke 14:28-30 - [28]"Suppose one of you wants to build a tower. Will he not first sit down and estimate the cost to see if he has enough money to complete it? [29]For if he lays the foundation and is not able to finish it, everyone who sees it will ridicule him, [30]saying, 'This fellow began to build and was not able to finish.'

II Timothy 2:15 - [15]Do your best to present yourself to God as one approved, a workman who does not need to be ashamed and who correctly handles the word of truth.

Proverbs 1:7 - [7] The fear of the LORD is the beginning of knowledge, but fools despise wisdom and discipline.

Proverbs 6:8 - [8] yet it stores its provisions in summer and gathers its food at harvest.

Proverbs 24:27 - [27] Finish your outdoor work and get your fields ready; after that, build your house.

Psalm 119-99-100 - [99] I have more insight than all my teachers, for I meditate on your statutes. [100] I have more understanding than the elders, for I obey your precepts.

Philippians 4:13 - [13] I can do everything through him who gives me strength.

Hebrews 12:1 - [1] Therefore, since we are surrounded by such a great cloud of witnesses, let us throw off everything that hinders and the sin that so easily entangles, and let us run with perseverance the race marked out for us.

Facing Finances

Psalm 24:1 - [1] The earth is the LORD's, and everything in it, the world, and all who live in it;

Matthew 6:24 - [24] "No one can serve two masters. Either he will hate the one and love the other, or he will be devoted to the one and despise the other. You cannot serve both God and Money.

Psalm 50:10-12 - [10] for every animal of the forest is mine, and the cattle on a thousand hills. [11] I know every bird in the mountains, and the creatures of the field are mine. [12] If I were hungry I would not tell you, for the world is mine, and all that is in it.

Ecclesiastes 5:10 - [10] Whoever loves money never has money enough; whoever loves wealth is never satisfied with his income. This too is meaningless.

Proverbs 21:20 - [20] In the house of the wise are stores of choice food and oil, but a foolish man devours all he has.

Matthew 25:23 - [23] "His master replied, 'Well done, good and faithful servant! You have been faithful with a few things; I will put you in charge of many things. Come and share your master's happiness!'

Luke 19:17 - [17] "'Well done, my good servant!' his master replied. 'Because you have been trustworthy in a very small matter, take charge of ten cities.'

Psalm 37:21 - [21] The wicked borrow and do not repay, but the righteous give generously;

Proverbs 3:28 - [28] Do not say to your neighbor, "Come back later; I'll give it tomorrow"— when you now have it with you.

Proverbs 22:7 - [27] Her house is a highway to the grave, leading down to the chambers of death.

Luke 12:22-32 - [22] Then Jesus said to his disciples: "Therefore I tell you, do not worry about your life, what you will eat; or about your body, what you will wear. [23] Life is more than food, and the body more than clothes. [24] Consider the ravens: They do not sow or reap, they have no storeroom or barn; yet God feeds them. And how much more valuable you are than birds! [25] Who of you by worrying can add a single hour to his life[a]? [26] Since you cannot do this very little thing, why do you worry about the rest?

[27] "Consider how the lilies grow. They do not labor or spin. Yet I tell you, not even Solomon in all his splendor was dressed like one of these. [28] If that is how God clothes the grass of the field, which is here today, and tomorrow is thrown into the fire, how much more will he clothe you, O you of little faith! [29] And do not set your heart on what you will eat or drink; do not worry about it. [30] For the pagan world runs after all such things, and your Father knows that you need them. [31] But seek his kingdom, and these things will be given to you as well. [32] "Do not be afraid, little flock, for your Father has been pleased to give you the kingdom.

Romans 13:7 - [7] Give everyone what you owe him: If you owe taxes, pay taxes; if revenue, then revenue; if respect, then respect; if honor, then honor.

Proverbs 22:26-27 - [26] Do not be a man who strikes hands in pledge or puts up security for debts; [27] if you lack the means to pay, your very bed will be snatched from under you.

Proverbs 3:5-6 - [5] Trust in the LORD with all your heart and lean not on your own understanding; [6] in all your ways acknowledge him, and he will make your paths straight.

Proverbs 3:9-10 - [9] Honor the LORD with your wealth, with the first fruits of all your crops; [10] then your barns will be filled to overflowing, and your vats will brim over with new wine.

Proverbs 10:22 - [22] The blessing of the LORD brings wealth, and he adds no trouble to it.

Galatians 6:7 - [7]Do not be deceived: God cannot be mocked. A man reaps what he sows.

Proverbs 21:20 - [20] In the house of the wise are stores of choice food and oil, but a foolish man devours all he has.

Ecclesiastes 11:2 - [2] Give portions to seven, yes to eight, for you do not know what disaster may come upon the land.

Malachi 3:10 - [10] Bring the whole tithe into the storehouse, that there may be food in my house. Test me in this," says the LORD Almighty, "and see if I will not throw open the floodgates of heaven and pour out so much blessing that you will not have room enough for it.

Luke 6:38 - [38]Give, and it will be given to you. A good measure, pressed down, shaken together and running over, will be poured into your lap. For with the measure you use, it will be measured to you."

I Corinthians 16:1-3 - [1]Now about the collection for God's people: Do what I told the Galatian churches to do. [2]On the first day of every week, each one of you should set aside a sum of money in keeping with his income, saving it up, so that when I come no collections will have to be made. [3]Then, when I arrive, I will give letters of introduction to the men you approve and send them with your gift to Jerusalem.

Proverbs 13:22 - [22] A good man leaves an inheritance for his children's children, but a sinner's wealth is stored up for the righteous.

Acts 10:2 - [2]He and all his family were devout and God-fearing; he gave generously to those in need and prayed to God regularly.

Exploring the World

Matthew 28:19 - [19]Therefore go and make disciples of all nations, baptizing them in[a] the name of the Father and of the Son and of the Holy Spirit…

Mark 16:15 - [15]He said to them, "Go into all the world and preach the good news to all creation.

Matthew 13:38 - [38]The field is the world, and the good seed stands for the sons of the kingdom. The weeds are the sons of the evil one…

Psalm 96:3 - [3] Declare his glory among the nations, his marvelous deeds among all peoples.

Matthew 24:14 - [14]And this gospel of the kingdom will be preached in the whole world as a testimony to all nations, and then the end will come., **28:19 -** [19]Therefore go and make disciples of all nations, baptizing them in[a] the name of the Father and of the Son and of the Holy Spirit…

Mark 16:15 - [15]He said to them, "Go into all the world and preach the good news to all creation.

Luke 24:47 - [47]and repentance and forgiveness of sins will be preached in his name to all nations, beginning at Jerusalem.

Colossians 3:12 - [12]Therefore, as God's chosen people, holy and dearly loved, clothe yourselves with compassion, kindness, humility, gentleness and patience.

I Peter 2:5-7 - [5]you also, like living stones, are being built into a spiritual house to be a holy priesthood, offering spiritual sacrifices acceptable to God through Jesus Christ. [6]For in Scripture it says: "See, I lay a stone in Zion, a chosen and precious cornerstone, and the one who trusts in him will never be put to shame." [7]Now to you who believe, this stone is precious. But to those who do not believe, "The stone the builders rejected has become the capstone…"

Ephesians 6:7 - [7]Serve wholeheartedly, as if you were serving the Lord, not men…

Luke 12:48 - [8]But the one who does not know and does things deserving punishment will be beaten with few blows. From everyone who has been given much, much will be demanded; and from the one who has been entrusted with much, much more will be asked., **19:13** - [13]So he called ten of his servants and gave them ten minas. [a]'Put this money to work,' he said, 'until I come back.'

I Corinthians 4:2 - [2]Now it is required that those who have been given a trust must prove faithful., **6:20** - [20]you were bought at a price. Therefore honor God with your body.

Proverbs 24:21 - [21] Fear the LORD and the king, my son, and do not join with the rebellious, **14:34** - [34] Righteousness exalts a nation, but sin is a disgrace to any people.

Matthew 22:21 - [21]"Caesar's," they replied. Then he said to them, "Give to Caesar what is Caesar's, and to God what is God's."

Romans 13:1 - [1]Everyone must submit himself to the governing authorities, for there is no authority except that which God has established. The authorities that exist have been established by God.

Titus 3:1 - [1]Remind the people to be subject to rulers and authorities, to be obedient, to be ready to do whatever is good…

Acts 23:5 - [5]Paul replied, "Brothers, I did not realize that he was the high priest; for it is written: 'Do not speak evil about the ruler of your people.'"

Parting Words

Psalm 37:25-26 - "I was young and now I am old, yet I have never seen the righteous forsaken or their children begging bread. They are always generous and lend freely; their children will be blessed."

APPENDIX B – EXAMPLES

• •

Vision statements are statements that tell what you want to create for the future. It is usually a sentence or two (may be more) that indicate in general terms what is foreseen for the future. It is what all have agreed that you will work towards achieving.

Sample Vision Statements

Sample 1 - Our family will improve the world through a genuine desire to better the lives of others by demonstrating care and concern for all.

Sample 2 – We will transform a group of individuals who are related by blood, marriage, and/or adoption into a productive and functioning family unit.

Sample 3 – Our family will create an environment that provides for the proper growth and development of all members through loving, planning, and working together to fulfill God's purpose for our lives.

Mission statements give the purpose for being. They help families identify their purpose.

Sample Mission Statements

Sample 1 - We will love:
- God
- All man/woman kind
- Nature
- Pure and positive thoughts and ideas

Sample 2 – As a family, we will show God's love through kindness, love, and a spirit of hospitality.

Sample 3 – We exist to 1) worship God; 2) love one another; and to serve man/woman kind.

Sample 4 – We will seek God's guidance in all we do. We will walk in love toward our fellow man/woman. We will practice forgiveness toward others. We will model honesty and integrity. We will seek peace and reject injustice.

The Intentional Parenting Plan

Developed by
Dr. Veda Pendleton McClain, Ph.D.

The Intentional Parenting Plan
Prepared for

_____

By _____

As the parent(s) of _____, I (We) have prayed about her/his life and have decided that I (We) want the following for this child.

Shaping, Character, Conduct, and Conversation

I (we) want _____ to experience the _____ faith

and believe _____. We will

make sure that this happens by _____.

Daily habits that we will encourage in the faith are:

1.

2.

3.

4.

5.

The values that are most important for my child to develop are:

1.

2.

3.

Biblical goals for this child include:

Character:

    1.

    2.

    3.

Conduct:

    1.

    2.

    3.

Conversation:

    1.

    2.

    3.

_____ has the following gifts that need to be encouraged and developed.

1.

2.

3.

I (we) will talk openly and honestly to _____ about

    - sex at age _____

    - female/male relationships and dating at age _____

    - substance use and abuse at age _____

    - death and dying at age _____

    - marriage at age _____

This child will be disciplined using _____ ,

_____ , and _____ . Her/his "free

will" will be shaped by _____ and _____ .

_____ will have to learn to do the following chores at home.

_____ Dust	_____ Empty trash	_____ sweep
_____ Wash dishes	_____ Vacuum	_____ Wash clothes
_____ Clean room	_____ Fold laundry	_____ Clean kitchen
_____ Clean bathroom	_____ Mop	_____ Cook
_____ Make bed	_____ Yard work	_____ Other

We (I) will show love by _____ and _____ .

She/he will learn to show gratitude by _____ .

She/he will be shown how to care for others by _____ and

_____ .

Manners will be learned by _____ .

Rewards for obedience will include _____ , _____ ,

and _____ .

_____ must understand _____

about her/his attitude, and _____

about her/his aptitude.

When facing tough times, we (I) will offer support by _____

and _____ .

Image

The three most important factors to encourage _____ in developing

her/his image will be:

1.

2.

3.

_____ will wear _____ clothing based on

_____ . We (I) will help in choosing these

clothes by _____ .

Her/his general appearance will be _____ because it will

help her/him become _____ .

At home, _____ will learn how to:

_____ cook	_____ clean	_____ build	_____ iron
_____ organize	_____ bake	_____ plan	_____ wash
_____ mow lawn	_____ paint	_____ repair car	_____ sweep
_____ create	_____ sew		

We (I) want _____ to get to know and love _____

(family members) and will make sure that happens by _____ .

_____ will get the following vaccinations.

_____ all recommended by physician   _____ childhood diseases only

_____ Gardisil   _____ None at all

We will plan for weekly meals by _____. Our diets will include

_____.

_____ will have the following for school lunches.

_____ cafeteria food   _____ take lunch from home

_____ fast food if allowed   _____ processed food from stores

Our family will participate in physical activities such as _____,

_____, and _____ to help us maintain healthy

bodies on a _____ daily or _____ weekly basis.

_____ will participate in these school or after school activities.

1.

2.

3.

4.

5.

Dr. _____ is our pediatrician and he/she can be reached at

_____. Our family doctor is _____ and can be reached

at _____. In the event that neither can be reached, an alternate

physician is _____ and can be reached at _____.

Other physicians that _____ sees include:

Allergist _____Phone _____

Ear, nose and throat _____Phone _____

Dentist _____ Phone _____

Optometrist _____ Phone _____

Orthopedic surgeon _____ Phone _____

Dermatologist _____ Phone _____

Gynecologist _____ Phone _____

Urologist _____ Phone _____

Orthodontist _____ Phone _____

Psychiatrist _____ Phone _____

Home remedies that we want to use include:

_____ for _____

_____ for _____

_____ for _____

Home Life

Influential people for our family include:

1.   2.

2.   4.

Our family will live in a _____ in _____, _____.

The most important rules for our home are:

1.

2.

3.

4.

The daily schedule for _____ will be:

Fun activities will include:

1.

2.

3.

We will learn to laugh by:

1.

2.

3.

We will listen to _____ and _____ music.

The games we will learn to play are:

1.

2.

3.

_____ should know the following about our family history and culture:

Privacy policies for _____ will be:

Parenting

_____ is our spiritual leader and he/she can be reached

at _____. In the event he/she is unavailable, _____

can be reached at _____ for comfort and guidance.

The following people have agreed to stand by us as we rear this child.

1.

2.

3.

The following books will be read in order to stay motivated and gain strength and

wisdom.

1.

2.

3.

List others you plan to contact for wise counsel.

_____ is expected to do the following on a daily basis.

1.

2.

3.

The final authority in decision making in our home will be _____.

In the event of my (our) untimely death, _____ will

live with _____ until she/he reaches majority.

The alternate guardian will be _____. Should temporary

guardianship become necessary in the case of illness or my (our) absence,

_____ will live with _____.

My (our) will and insurance policies and other important papers are located in

_____.

In the event of an emergency, please contact _____ at phone

_____, email _____, and address

_____.

The following family heirlooms will be passed on to _____.

Memorable sayings that this child should know are :

1.

2.

3.

Education

I (we) plan to assist with the education of this child by:

1.

2.

3.

I (we) will participate in school activities by:

1.

2.

3.

_____ will take part in the following extracurricular activities:

1.

2.

3.

I (we) will show that education is important by _____.

The potential careers for _____ are _____,

_____, and _____.

_____ shows signs of having the following gifts and talents that

need to be cultivated:

1.

2.

3.

_____ will attend _____ public/private school or

will be home schooled.

After high school, it would be ideal for _____ to attend

_____ . It will be paid for by

_____ .

As _____ grows, she/he will participate in these after school

activities:

1.

2.

3.

_____ will be encouraged to read:

1.

2.

3.

If help is needed with school concerns or school work, we will contact

_____ and _____ for assistance.

If grade retention, social promotion, or skipping a grade becomes an issue for

_____ , I (we) do/do not want that for her/him.

Assistance in the event of special needs will be sought at _____ .

I (we) will communicate with teachers by _____ .

I (we) will work on literacy skills at home by doing the following:

1.

2.

3.

Homework will be monitored by _____ .

The homework policy for our home will be

_____ .

_____ will be encouraged to participate in education related

activities such as:

1.

2.

3.

Facing Finances

_____ will learn _____ about

spending money. _____ will also learn the following about:

Saving –

Giving –

Investing –

The three most important financial investments I (we) will make for _____

are

Investment	Cost	Source
1.		
2.		
3.		

_____ will/will not have an allowance. It will be _____ per week/month.

_____ will learn _____ about budgeting.

I (we) want _____ to inherit _____

about handling finances.

Our vacation spots will include:

1.

2.

3.

She/he will learn _____ from visiting these locations.

_____ will be taught to care for the poor and needy by

_____.

Exploring the World

Service activities that will be important for _____ to complete are

Activity   How I (we) will support these activities

1.

2.

3.

4.

5.

I (we) would like to see _____ travel to _____

because _____ .

I (we) will support world missions by _____ .

It will be important for _____ to participate in the following

community activities:

1.

2.

3.

I (we) will teach _____ the following about other races, cultures, etc."

1.

2.

3.

I (we) will encourage involvement in the following civic activities:

1.

2.

3.

_____ will learn about caring for the environment by

_____ .

Leadership skills will be developed in _____ by _____

_____ .

List other hopes and desires that you have for _____ . Tell

how you will work to make them happen.

This document is our written plan for the life of _____.

I (we) believe that this is God's design for her/his life and my/our signature(s) below indicates our desires for this child's life. This plan is to be followed as long as we live and/or in the event of our untimely death, incapacitation, illness, or other situations that make us unavailable for making clear and effective decisions.

_____   _____
Parent   Date

_____   _____
Parent   Date

_____   _____
Witness   Date

_____   _____
Witness   Date

_____   _____
Witness   Date

In witness whereof I hereunto set my hand and official seal.

_____
Notary

_____   _____
County   State

My Commission Expires:_____

Glossary of Terms

● ● ● ● ● ● ● ● ● ● ● ● ● ● ● ● ● ● ● ●

Adversity – an unfavorable act that goes against what one desires.

Career - a person's professional life; a vocation with the potential for growth

College – an institution of higher education; either a 2-year or 4-year institution

Denomination – a particular religious group with several churches

Fruit of the Spirit – Galatians 5:22-23; "But the fruit of the Spirit is love, joy, peace, patience, kindness, goodness, faithfulness, gentleness and self-control.

Going green – beginning to become concerned about the environment and taking steps to protect it through conservation efforts.

Heirlooms – a family gift that can be passed down from one generation to the next.

Holy Communion – the elements of bread and wine used to celebrate the death of Jesus Christ.

Human sexuality – having the traits of sex

Humor – funny or amusing

Inclusion – in schools, the act of including children of varying abilities in the same classroom for instruction.

Integrity –abiding by certain moral principles that reflect good character

Liberal Arts college/university – a higher education institution that provides students with knowledge in the arts, social sciences, humanities, and sciences.

Mantras – a repeated phrase or slogan

Mission statement – a sentence that clearly defines the goals and purposes of an entity

Oral language skills – the ability to speak using words

Private college/university – a higher education institution funded by dollars from private (i.e. individuals, corporations) resources

Public college/university – a higher education institution funded by dollars from public resources (i.e. government)

Retention – keeping a student in a grade after a year in that grade; repeating a grade

Social promotion – sending a student to the next grade although the student has not mastered the material of the current grade

Self-control – being able to contain one's thoughts and actions

Temperance – self-control through moderation

Traits – a characteristic of one's nature

Vaccinations/Immunizations – an injection given to prevent disease

Vision – what one anticipates seeing in advance

Vocational/technical school – an institution that prepares students for a particular occupation in a technical field

Resources and Other Thinking Tools

Books

Chapman, G., The five love languages of children. Chicago: Northfield Publishing, 1997.

DeGaetano, G. Parent success stories. Seattle: Parent Coaching Institute, 2009.

Dobson, J. C., Parenting isn't for cowards. Dallas: Word Publishing, 1997.

Dobson, J. C. The strong-willed child. Wheaton: Tyndale House, 1992.

Dollar, C. A. & Dollar, T. L. (2002). The Successful Family: Everything you need to know to duild a stronger family. Atlanta: Crefic Dollar Ministries.

Omartian, S., The power of a praying parent. Eugene: Harvest House, 1995.

Miller, S. & B., Memory verse games for kids. Eugene: Harvest House, 1997.

Smith, G. E., The do's and don'ts of parenting. Chicago: Management Planning Institute, Inc. 2006.

Treat, C., Renewing the mind: The key to transformation. Tulsa: Harrison House, 1993.

Internet

Christian Parenting

http://www.allaboutparenting.org/christian-parenting.htm

Christian Parents

http://www.christian-parents.net/

Crosswalk

http://www.crosswalk.com/parenting/

Family Life Today

http://www.familylife.com/site/c.dnJHKLNnFoG/b.3082787/k.BF6A/Home.htm

Focus on the Family

http://www.focusonthefamily.com/

Intentional Living

http://www.theintentionallife.com/

Kids Source Online

http://www.kidsource.com/

MomSense

http://www.christianitytoday.com/momsense/

Positive Parenting

http://www.positiveparenting.com/

The Parent Coaching Institute

http://www.parentcoachinginstitute.com/

The Parent Institute

http://www.parent-institute.com/educator/

The Parent Place

http://www.tppos.org/

The Parents' Place

http://www.parentsplacefrc.com/

AUTHOR'S NOTE

● ● ● ● ● ● ● ● ● ● ● ● ● ● ● ● ● ● ● ●

The most important calling in my life has been that of being a parent. Although I have help positions in public schools and in higher education, the most fulfilling role for me has been that of being a mother to my five children. My children were the reasons for my going to work and pursuing positions that would allow me to adequately provide for them. They were the ones who kept me grounded and provided the daily reality check when things did not go well at work. And they were the ones who provided that unconditional love that I needed on so many occasions after a difficult day. I am truly blessed that God chose me to parent them. I will be eternally grateful to God and to them for the experiences I have had as a parent.

Each child brought to our family unique qualities that enhanced our home life. Their personalities are as distinct as the five fingers on my hand, but it was those personalities that wove us together as a functional and productive unit to face the everyday challenges of the world. Their individuality helped me better understand individual purpose and promise, as well as the need as a parent for me to value and shape each child toward her/his natural bent. Their differences also helped me become more effective as a parent and more purposeful in my prayer life about each child. As they grew physically and emotionally, I began to grow emotionally and spiritually. That spiritual growth is what has sustained me when tough times have come. It is my prayer that you too will be nurtured and developed emotionally and spiritually as you parent.

Veda McClain

ABOUT THE AUTHOR

• • • • • • • • • • • • • • • • • • • •

Dr. Veda Pendleton McClain's greatest calling has been that of being a parent. She is a Christian mother of five children and young adults and is a teacher, teacher educator, consultant, entrepreneur, and parenting coach. Most of her parenting years have been completed as a single parent.

A native of Pine Bluff, AR, Dr. McClain has taught in the public schools of Little Rock, AR, and in various institutions of higher education in Georgia and Arkansas. She has also served as a department and college administrator. Dr. McClain earned a bachelor of arts degree in English from Wesleyan University, a master of science in education degree in reading from the University of Central Arkansas, and a doctor of philosophy in reading education from the University of Georgia.

Dr. McClain is also the grandmother of five beautiful granddaughters and grandsons. She is currently a parenting coach, entrepreneur, and education consultant, and can be reached at veda_mcclain@yahoo.com. Visit www.vedamcclain.com for more information.

Writing from her own real-life experiences, Dr. McClain uses The Intentional Parenting Plan (TIPP) to share her insight into planning for child rearing from a Christian perspective. Using scriptures, parents will complete TIPP with a written plan to guide them in rearing their child.